THE JEWISH AGENDA

ESSAYS IN CONTEMPORARY JEWISH LIFE

DAVID J. SCHNALL

PRAEGER

New York
Westport, Connecticut
London

Library of Congress Cataloging-in-Publication Data

Schnall, David J.
  The Jewish agenda.

  Bibliography: p.
  Includes index.
    1. Jews—United States. 2. Judaism—United States.
3. Israel. 4. Judaism—Israel. 5. Zionism—United
States. 6. United States—Ethnic relations. I. Title
E184.J5S332 1987   973'.04924   87-11800
ISBN 0-275-92564-1 (alk. paper)

Library of Congress Catalog Card Number: 87-11800
ISBN: 0-275-92564-1

First published in 1987

Praeger Publishers, One Madison Avenue, New York, NY 10010
A division of Greenwood Press, Inc.

Printed in the United States of America

The paper used in this book complies with the
Permanent Paper Standard issued by the National
Information Standards Organization (Z39.48-1984).

10 9 8 7 6 5 4 3 2 1

TO TOVA,
ELIEZER, ETAN, AND YONINA—

only they understand

TO THE BLESSED MEMORIES OF
MILKAH ROTH AND ROCHEL SCHNALL,

two grand ladies

Contents

ACKNOWLEDGMENTS   ix

INTRODUCTION   xi

Part One   America: The Land of Promise

1   The Game of Jewish Demography   3

2   Out of the Faith   17

3   Orthodoxy Resurgent   31

4   Republicans, Democrats, and U.S. Jews   51

Part Two   Israel: The Promised Land

5   Haredim and Emunim: Religious Extremism
     and Israeli Life   67

6   Settlers from the New World   85

7   The Insoluble Dilemma   101

Part Three   Zionism: Keeping the Promise Alive

8   American Zionism: Continuity and Change   121

9   Yordim: Zionism in Reverse   137

10   Whither Soviet Jewry?   153

viii   Contents

BIBLIOGRAPHY   173
INDEX   181
ABOUT THE AUTHOR   187

Acknowledgments

In any project as broad and extensive as this, there are numerous individuals who contribute time and effort from the first conceptualization to the finished product. It is impossible to acknowledge all to whom thanks are due. Invariably some are omitted. For this I apologize in advance.

There are several, however, who must be mentioned for their special contributions. First is my good friend and mentor, Dr. Carl Figliola, University Dean of the Faculty of Business, Public Administration, and Accountancy of Long Island University. Carl's foremost commitment is to his faculty. He provides the personal encouragement and professional atmosphere within which creative accomplishment is possible.

In addition, gratitude must also be extended to the Faculty Research Committee of Long Island University and the administration of its C. W. Post Campus. Without the generous support and sabbatical leave they provided, this volume would never have been completed.

My thanks also go to the many people who were instrumental in the research and revision of this book. This includes the editors of several journals who initially published the work from which some of these essays were derived: *Judaism*, *Midstream*, the *National Jewish Monthly*, *Newsday Magazine*, and *Tradition*. Thanks are extended to Mrs. Karen Leon who helped index the manuscript.

In the course of the writing, I had the opportunity to interview numerous individuals, both specialists and everyday folk. The insights I gleaned from them and the friendships that resulted are an integral part of this volume and its satisfactions. In an important sense the book is as much theirs as it is mine.

A note of gratitude is also due to Mr. and Mrs. Harry Schnall and Rabbi and Mrs. Solomon Shoulson for their enthusiastic support, encouragement, and guidance. We may not always agree about the Jewish agenda, but as parents they are exemplary and their commitment to family emerges in everything they say or do.

Finally, there is no way that I can adequately express the contributions of my wife and children toward the completion of this very personal project. They have sacrificed mightily on its behalf. Their love, loyalty, and devotion serve as inspiration for all my endeavors. Without them, it just wouldn't be worthwhile.

Introduction

I

Modern Jewish folklore has made much of Chelm, once an actual town in Eastern Europe. Said to be inhabited by fools and simpletons, it was a place that lived by an inside-out logic all its own. Consequently, residents believed that only they had a genuine grasp of things.

Myth has it that the Lord summoned a particular angel for a very special mission. He had mustered a sack of foolish souls and charged the angel with distributing them among the various localities of the world. But alas, the messenger was no Rhodes scholar himself. Once dispatched, he got caught in a storm and lost his way.

Flying in poor visibility, he ultimately bumped his head on a passing cloud and dropped his payload. As a result, his entire cargo landed within the municipal borders of Chelm, marking it for ever after as a village of fools.

The story goes that two elders of Chelm were stooped beneath a street lamp late one night, searching, searching. A third happened upon them. "What are you fellows doing?" he asked innocently, anxious to be of help.

One of the two looked up. "His wife," he said, pointing to his companion, "lost her diamond engagement ring." The other grunted. "And we're trying to see if we can find it before it gets light and the street gets real busy."

"Oh," said the passerby. "Did she lose it here?"

"No," the man replied, slightly annoyed. "She lost it around the corner, down the alleyway—you know, near the garbage can."

"So," came the inevitable query, delivered in the singsong tones of the Talmudic study hall, "if she lost it around the corner, down the alleyway, near the garbage can, why are you searching here?"

The two stood up to their full height and looked their questioner straight in the eye. "Don't you understand anything?" they said as one. "We're searching here—because this is where the light is!"

Though apocryphal, the little vignette says much to those of us in the business of evaluating social and political trends and offering generalizations based upon them. We spend a great deal of time looking "where the light is." It's safer, less confusing, and more straightforward. We have a good idea of what things are and what they are not, and if we find something of interest, we can easily assess just what it is.

But as a result, we don't often find much jewelry. The diamond engagement rings tend to be hidden "down the alleyway, near the garbage can." Finding them requires that we sift through the muck and mire. Worse yet, when we do find something, it's not at all clear that what looks valuable in the dark of night will be anything more than a worthless old boot by light of day.

Still, the mission remains for those who don't mind getting their hands dirty, and that mission is very much what influenced the writing of this book. In the coming pages we will explore the muck and the mire as it relates to the Jewish present and immediate future. We will consider some of the most pressing issues for contemporary Jewish life from a variety of perspectives, and we will evaluate some of the suggestions that have been made for overcoming its most important confrontations.

Invariably, in undertaking so weighty a task, two criticisms are raised. They are easy comments, attractive to reviewers even if they have given the work only passing notice. The one I dub the "what about Fred?" syndrome. The other may be called the "but my brother-in-law" factor.

The former is essentially an error of omission. In approaching a presentation as broad as this, some reader will rise to object, opening his volley with, "What about Fred?" He will then detail the problems of an acquaintance whose needs are equally pressing yet not included within the binding of this work. If such dire considerations are omitted from the volume, then it fails in its mission to be inclusive, the objection implies.

To suggest directly or indirectly that this presentation incorporates every possible item on the contemporary "Jewish agenda" or on the emerging agenda of the next decade is presumptuous and arrogant. The author has drawn a list of priorities that may not include the personal or communal needs of all those who fall beneath the umbrella of Jewish life and culture. To some degree the effort must be subjective and arbitrary in what it says and in what it leaves out.

In addition, there are topics that have been confronted as part of a broader field rather than as full chapters or major subsections. Consequently, it would be well for those who raise this objection to consult the index carefully. Still—for all the Freds among my readers—I apologize in advance and hope that what has been omitted will find its way into the sequel to this work, already in the early stages of planning.

By contrast, the "but my brother-in-law" factor is more an error of commission. It occurs to the reader who finds some broad generalization offensive. Essentially, the objections are based on the fact that his brother-in-law (or any other friend, relative, associate, or neighbor) simply does not fit the mold.

There may be several variables at work here, some independent and others in combination. First, any generalizations are exactly that. They attempt to draw broad-based conclusions, to discern meaningful trends from the aggregate experiences of the many. A substantial minority may conform to a lesser degree, if at all.

In addition, there is a profound concern deep in the heart of any author, particularly one undertaking a work such as this. International initiatives, social trends, and personal predilections are dynamic variables that often seem to undergo radical redirection, at least in the short term. There is always the fear that the analysis of any issue, much less ten major ones, will appear obsolete before the ink is dry. To overcome some of that, emphasis here is generally on the broad stroke rather than the specific, when possible. Still, the problem remains.

Finally, some of the data that form the basis of these essays are quantitative—interpreted and digested by the author. This in itself will be less than fascinating to many readers, and in some corners of the

Jewish community, the very methodology is suspect; nevertheless, it is the stuff of which much social analysis is made. Perhaps the suspicions result from an age-old aversion to being counted. Biblical and Talmudic writ have linked plague and pestilence to the envy and jealousy accompanying direct census, and the Talmud explains that blessings can accrue only to things that remain unnumbered.

Certain sectors of the Jewish community may feel that such presentations are too often commissioned by their social or religious adversaries. Consequently, they fear they are underestimated, their numbers or their import devalued accidentally or by design. As a result of all this, some of the data and their interpretations are indeed erroneous, though well intentioned. So to all the "brothers-in-law" who read this volume, once again, I apologize in advance.

II

This book has resulted from the convergence of several related effects. On the one hand, it is very much the outgrowth of my own personality and development. I have been trained in the rabbinate and in the social sciences: at once teaching Judaic subjects alongside the more traditional liberal arts, at once concerned with ethnic and social trends from both a moral and professional perspective, at once operating as a consultant to Jewish social and academic organizations as well as to organizations of secular and general orientation.

The confluence has not always been a happy one. Among academics I have long been a rabbi, to much concerned with the impact and ramifications of events and trends, too little detached in the yen for the ultimate statistical model. Among rabbis, by contrast, I have long been an academic, too much concerned with the elegance of methodology and analysis, too little driven by the forces of the "real world."

My experience planted the desire to produce a work that is more than a composite of political/social currents yet less than a sermonic or homiletic exercise. It should be broad enough to cover much that currently confronts the Jewish community, yet deep enough to satisfy both the specialist and the intelligent lay person in its detail and in its analysis.

The mission is an awesome one. In short, the work must remain true to proper political or sociological evaluation yet engage a general readership for whom the dry presentation of quantitative, or even qualitative, data means little. In that regard, the pages that follow are profoundly personal.

The work did not emerge from a comprehensive whole, however. Rather, the essays presented here stem from several sources. Some are based on lectures presented at various conferences, campuses, or community programs over the past several years. In particular, the first section of this volume had its genesis from encounters with Jews and Jewish communities of all religious, social, and cultural types. Indeed, such lecture tours and personal interaction are among the most satisfying of all my professional activities.

In addition, many of the essays are based on my own previous publications, both scholarly and popular. In these cases the work was recast, expanded, and updated for publication here. Several were combined and revised so extensively that they were almost unrecognizable to the editors who were kind enough to publish them initially. In that sense, their presentation here is both old and new. Nevertheless, permission has been requested and credit noted in the acknowledgments.

The book is divided into three parts, creating parameters for the essays found therein. These, in turn, mirror much of what makes up the contemporary Jewish experience: life in the United States, the renewal of Jewish statehood, and the relationship between the two in the form of Zionist ideology.

The first part deals with Jewish life in the United States. Here chapters are dedicated to sociological, religious, and political currents and the mix between them. In each case, some social history is injected to lend perspective to the discussions and to allow individual readers to match the harder data with their own experiences or the experiences of those close to them.

Demographic issues, the role of women, and projections about contemporary Jewish family life are evaluated in the first two chapters. Anecdotes that illustrate the point have been included here and elsewhere, in the further hope of translating some of these broad generalizations into the realm of the personal.

The third deals with the emergence of an Orthodox community in the United States that is far different from its predecessors and from the assumptions made about it a generation ago. The social backgrounds of the development, its strengths, and its weaknesses are all considered within this context.

The subject of the final chapter in this section is the electoral and

political future of the U.S. Jewish community under both Republican
and Democratic administrations. It evaluates both domestic and international concerns and sets the Jewish propensity toward political liberalism into historical perspective.

In the second part, the focus of the work shifts from the United
States to Israel. Here three social and political developments are given
consideration among the myriad issues that could easily have been
included. The first chapter deals with unrest among religious communities in Israel. The subject has recently gained international interest
as violence among Jews in Israel and between observant Jews and
Arabs has been broadcast in the foreign and domestic media. The matter has always been an undercurrent of life in a nation that links gov-
ernmental and theological elites in the face of deep popular divisions
over the role of religion in politics and daily life.

The second chapter confronts the question of *aliyah*, the migration
of Jews from their residences in the Diaspora to Israel, the ancestral
homeland. Since the creation of the state, aliyah has been a primary
objective of Zionism as both an ideology and a political movement.
Yet it has met with little success among Jews of the Western world.

This essay considers the needs and interests of a particular group of
those who have emigrated from the United States to live not only in
Israel but in the disputed territories. Its intention is to offer reflections
of Israeli life broadly, and pioneering settlement specifically, as it is
encountered by immigrants. Both interviews and anecdotes are used to
reflect on the enterprise of aliyah.

The third essay in this part relates to one of the most troublesome
aspects of contemporary Jewish life in Israel. It evaluates the prospects
of coexistence with Israel's large mass of Arab residents, especially
since the conquests of 1967 and the international stalemates thereafter.
Given the demographic, military, and diplomatic facets of this issue,
many have termed it Israel's ''insoluble dilemma''—hence the chapter
title.

The final part is an attempt to draw links between the U.S. Jewish
community and its Israeli brethren in the form of political Zionism.
But, as in the pages before it, the emphasis here is less on theory and
ideology than on the issues that Zionism must confront as a movement. In the first chapter, the focus returns to the social and political
trends already noted in regard to U.S. Jewry. My intention here, how-

ever, is to assess their impact upon the support for and attachment to the Jewish homeland among America's Jews.

The following chapter takes its cue from the earlier one dealing with aliyah and Americans in Israel. Its emphasis, however, turns the concept on its head to detail *yerida*, the out-migration of Israelis to the United States. Their hopes, aspirations, and conflicts, as well as the frustrations of U.S. and Israeli leaders over the matter, are presented as a contrast to the formal ideology that Zionism represents.

Of course, Zionism calls for the "ingathering of the exiles" from all the lands of their dispersion. With that in mind, the final essay is dedicated to one of the most confusing and courageous chapters of contemporary Jewish life: the movement in support of human rights and free migration for the Jews of the Soviet Union.

The complicated and often conflicting aspects of human rights policy are detailed and evaluated alongside the personal decisions of those who have been permitted to emigrate. My intent, once again, is more than narrative. My hope is to set the events and their ramifications within the context of Zionist ideology, particularly as it is practiced by Israeli political figures and leaders of the U.S. Jewish community.

To be sure, individual topics could have been just as easily included under an alternative rubric. Inevitably, at least to some degree, such decisions are arbitrary. The chapters have been arranged in this fashion to lend clarity to the volume as a whole and to make it more accessible to readers with varied interests. The reader who objects to this arrangement is invited to choose those topics and sections that interest him or her most. No priority is implied in the presentation. In fact, the book was not written in the order of its presentation, so there is no reason to read it that way.

Finally, in a work of this sort, bias must inevitably emerge. The topics are too important and the passions too profound for it to be otherwise. There are personal and organizational loyalties at stake here, and such commitments tend to be deep and of long standing. I would be disappointed, therefore, if no one were to be offended by my assertions and conclusions.

With all this in mind, I have made an attempt to balance my presentation but not to hide my own orientations. I am a member of the Orthodox Jewish community who has spent much of his life studying, teaching, writing, and thinking about the contemporary Jewish condition. I am committed to traditional Judaism, to Zionism, and to the State of Israel, and I seek the continued vitality and success of Jewish life no matter where it may be resident.

My belief is that these objectives are best served by an open, calm, and candid consideration of the issues and options that present themselves. The calm and candor must predominate over the divisive personal and organizational stakes noted above. I can only hope that my meager talents will make some contribution toward that end. If controversy is raised as a result, I welcome the opportunity to engage my critics over the issues. I ask only that we be permitted to conclude our debate by agreeing to disagree.

PART ONE

America: The Land of Promise

1

The Game of Jewish Demography

I

My grandmother passed away recently. A vital and active person, she had been intimately involved in the rearing of all her grandchildren. Her mind remained sharp and clear into her nineties, though her health failed her at the end.

Among my very special memories, I particularly treasure her talks with me about "the old days." She was a living bit of social history and a storehouse of information regarding the East European Jewish deluge that arrived here at the turn of the century. She, in turn, loved to recount her experiences as an immigrant on Manhattan's fabled lower Eastside, where she arrived at the tender age of eight.

Her father was sent ahead to find a job and prepare proper living quarters for his wife and six children. As soon as he was settled, he would arrange for the rest of the family to take up residence in this new golden land. It was all understood.

Luckily, my great-grandfather—for whom I was named—was an honorable man. More than a few in his position simply forgot that they had families, made arrangements for themselves, and began life anew. Later, having heard nothing from their husbands, women with their small children ventured to America on their own. They became the pitiful widows and orphans of the living.

This was not the case for my grandmother. Her father summoned the family after some six months and they prepared to make the long journey to "Columbus's country." I remember asking her how she was told to prepare for the journey. She knit her wrinkled brow.

"I really don't remember too much," she told me with a smile that reflected the years of experience and recollection that she assembled for our conversation. "But one thing stands out clearly. They told me that if I'm going to America I'd better be sure to take a shovel and a pail."

A shovel and a pail? I looked at her incredulously. She smiled again, this time in an almost patronizing sort of way. "Of course," she said, as if I had asked the most foolish of questions. "Everybody knew that when you got off the boat at Ellis Island or Castle Garden [the two immigrant processing centers in New York] there would be gold lying in the streets and diamonds on the branches of every tree. Without a pail and shovel, you'd miss out!"

As I reflect on these and other precious memories of this dear lady, the story seems quaint and naive. Yet there are still thousands of immigrants arriving on these shores with similar, if less imaginative, fantasies about the land of opportunity. If the story seems quaint and naive, so too was it dishonest and cruel. It indicated the blind aspirations and pride of those on both sides of the ocean.

In part it was fashioned by the desire to conjure a life diametrically opposed to the poverty and repression of Eastern Europe. The Jewish immigrants had suffered from within and from without. There was brutality imposed upon them outside their communities in the form of official repression linked to the anti-Semitic venom of the mob. This was translated into semiofficial pogroms and riots that violated their persons and property.

Truth be told, they were also subject to overbearing social structure from within. Idealization in the form of musical theater or award-winning fiction can never reverse the substance of a *shtetl* life that was laced by ignorance, superstition, and a heavy-handed caste mentality. One born to neither wealth nor scholarship could not hope for even the spiritual riches that Jewish religious life might offer the downtrodden.

From these shores, the myth was fashioned by relatives who arrived in advance but found no gold in the streets. Surely they couldn't admit to the failure of their fantasy. So with each letter home, their success and status was exaggerated still further until the poor reader had no choice but to make the move himself. After all, he had a rich cousin in America.

Of course, the immigrants of the last century found neither jewels nor riches lying in the street. But what they did find was equally valuable: an atmosphere untrammeled by the harsh, exclusionary cultural and social baggage that they knew all too well; one within which they were relatively free to apply their talents competitively.

This they turned to gold. Within the short space of three or four generations, the U.S. Jewish community has succeeded beyond the wildest dreams of its early arrivals. In effect, the grandchildren of those immigrants have struck the socioeconomic mother lode.

The following observations are based on studies published over the past few years. An analysis of family income by ethnic group found Jewish families to be the most affluent in the country, standing fully 72 percent above the national average. Families of Japanese descent, the runners-up in the survey, were about 40 percentage points behind.*

A national study on education conducted in the 1970s found that over 41 percent of Jewish males and over 24 percent of Jewish females had completed college. In both cases, this was roughly three times the national average. For Jewish males aged 30 to 39, the figures increased by over 60 percent. For Jewish females aged 30 to 39, the increase was 75 percent.

A more recent survey suggested thaht while Jewish males tend to be somewhat better educated than Jewish females, the gap is closing at around 60 percent college-educated, still well above the national average. It appears that we are not only affluent, but also extraordinarily well schooled.

High family income and an emphasis on university education have resulted in disproportionate numbers of Jewish men and women in upper-status professions and occupations. Thus 70 percent of Jewish males and about 40 percent of Jewish females hold such positions, putting both groups two to three times above the national figures. Among Jews between the ages of 30 and 39 the percentage is higher still, for both men and women.**

*Based on data compiled in Thomas Sowell, *Markets and Minorities* (New York: Basic Books, 1981).

**Unless otherwise noted, data cited here are based on those reported and analyzed in the *American Jewish Yearbook* over the past ten years. In addition, the author con-

II

There can be little doubt that U.S. Jews have found the gold of which my grandmother spoke. They have vaulted themselves into the upper reaches of U.S. society and quickly left their humble immigrant and proletarian roots behind. But like anything else in life, this momentous leap has not been without cost.

There are major challenges that face America's Jews—demographic, social, and cultural—that in many ways are the direct result of their great socioeconomic accomplishments. There may have been gold in the streets of America, but by no means was it free.

One confrontation revolves around the simple question of numbers. For the past several years, sociologists and demographers have issued stern warnings regarding the decline of the U.S. Jewish population. They have pointed to the inability—or more properly, the unwillingness—of America's Jews to produce sufficient offspring to assure even a stable population into the next century.

There are several factors that contribute to this decline. The most important is a steady drop in the Jewish birthrate, well below the replacement level. Demographers tell us that in order for a population to replace itself, it must produce 2.1 children per family (the additional tenth of a point for infants who die within their first months).

Various statistical studies, undertaken during the past decade, have asked Jewish couples how many children they have and how many they expect to have. In most cases, their reponses have not only tallied substantially below the numbers required for simple replacement, but they have been consistently lower than those of other religious groups.

For example, one study found that the average Jewish couple had borne 1.9 children at the time of the survey and expected to have 2.4 children in all. Both figures stand at least 10 percent below those gathered among Protestant couples and over 20 percent lower than the responses offered by Catholics.

While the average expectation of 2.4 children among Jews is comfortably above the replacement level, it is, after all, only an expectation. In child rearing as in life, actions speak louder than words.

sulted the demographic sections of Steven Cohen, *The 1984 National Survey of American Jews* (New York: American Jewish Committee, 1985) and Steven Cohen and Paul Ritterband, *Greater New York Jewish Population Study* (New York: Federation of Jewish Philanthropies of New York, 1983).

Perhaps most significant of all are the responses of Jewish couples under the age of 34, those of prime childbearing years. Here the average number of children born was 1.5, while the average number expected was 1.9—almost 10 percent below the replacement level. Younger couples are having fewer children than their elders did and fully expect to continue that trend throughout their childbearing years. According to a more recent study, these younger folks have fulfilled their intentions. The average number of children born to parents in the sample was 1.77, even lower than the average expected by younger couples in earlier studies. Demographers have given us cause to worry, purely in terms of the number of children born—and the number not.

Further, changes in the number of children born and in the pattern of birthrate have more than just numerical significance. They also have an impact on the way the Jewish community will be structured and the kinds of affiliations it can expect. For one thing, lower birthrates tend to increase the proportion of old to young in the population, a point to be examined below.

The increase of childless couples or those who have few children invariably will be reflected in organizational and synagogue membership, educational programming, and youth activities. In addition, the growing number of Jewish women in the workplace, particularly in professional pursuits, probably means that there will be fewer of them interested in the host of volunteer activities for which they are legend. Those who do participate are likely to be older than the volunteers of earlier decades.

The point is easily illustrated. Studies from the mid-1970s suggest that couples with no children are ten times less likely to exhibit high levels of Jewish organizational involvement than couples with children under the age of five. Similarly, couples with children under the age of fourteen are almost three times more likely to belong to a synagogue than those who have no children.

III

In many ways the falling birthrate, and all that it implies, is a tribute to the impact of the women's movement. Precisely because she is better educated than her mother, today's woman is far more likely to delay her marriage, at least until she has completed her education.

Bear in mind that this may well include a graduate or professional degree.

Once she has completed a rigorous course of professional training, it is unlikely that such a woman will simply turn her back on the labors of the past six or eight years in order to keep house. She may well decide to delay marriage still further so that she can pursue her career.

Even if she does marry toward the end or immediately upon the completion of her education, this does not imply the beginnings of a family. It is more likely that she will delay childbearing to practice her profession and to help build the family's resources for the future.

Consequently, today's professional, upwardly mobile young woman may very well marry or begin her family as much as ten years later than her mother did. It is probable that she follows this path with the blessings and encouragement of her mother, a woman who also perceives herself as enlightened and who may be fulfilling her own vicarious desires in the process.

It is ironic that the decision may prove more troublesome than imagined for both women. In the first instance, choosing a mate later and at a much more substantial life passage can make the choice difficult. A woman in U.S. society tends to marry "up," that is, to seek a mate who is better positioned—professionally, socially, and economically— than she is. As age increases, the number of available choices tends to decrease. Following some vague law of economics, demands increase while supply dwindles.

As a result, Jewish society has recently witnessed a bittersweet novelty: large numbers of singles—generally well educated and affluent, some divorced, most never married—trying to fit into the community, while ever seeking the perfect relationship.

But traditional community patterns are slow to adapt to new or passing realities. Jewish life has long been family centered, viewing the traditional unit as the most important single guarantor for the survival of the faith. Singles are viewed with equal helpings of suspicion, disdain, and pity. With rare exception, there is little room for these preeminent yuppies, much to the chagrin of the parents who encouraged them.

There has also been an almost humorous sidelight to the affair. Tired of blind dates or mindless social gatherings, these older and better educated singles, when they do choose to mate, have sought a better

way. Following the dictates of their professional training, many eschew the romantic mythology that has influenced U.S. social habits
for generations and reach out for something more rational.
Necessity is the mother of invention—or in this case, renewal. Though
still in its infancy, there has been an unmistakeable revival of the
shadchan, the Jewish matchmaker. As a current phenomenon, of course,
the institution has been revamped into a service that fits the model of
the 1980s. Yenta rides again—computer data base, videotapes, and
all.

So today's Jewish woman is likely to marry and have children a
great deal later (if at all) than did her mother. Further, following bio-
logic as well as socio-logic, today's Jewish woman will probably have
fewer children as well. The reasons are simple. Because she started
her childbearing later than her mother did, the contemporary Jewish
woman will probably have a far briefer period of fertility. She may
have a more difficult time conceiving her first child and each preg-
nancy will involve an increasing risk. Infertility and congenital defects
may be more common among women who begin their families later.

Feeling this pressure, some women (married or otherwise) rush to
have children "before it's too late." As a result, a small but notice-
able upward birth rate has been recorded, matching this race with the
biological time clock. This trend will likely be short-lived.

Further, because of professional commitments and aspirations, many
young Jewish women want to spend less time in raising the children
that they do have. The corporate road to the top is a long and arduous
one and not always tolerant of those who bow to personal demands.
Women are on the spot to disprove the sexist belief that even the
professionals among them see their careers as second to mothering and
family life.

This need not imply an unwillingness to invest in child rearing. It
does suggest, however, a willingness to entrust most of the child's
waking hours to the safekeeping of nurses, au pair, and sundry other
forms of live-in help. By contrast, maternal needs are to be satisfied
with a bare hour or two of "quality time" each day.

There are economic overtones as well. Because her married lifestyle
is likely to be upscale, requiring two professional incomes, there is a
sharp demand for the young Jewish mother to return to work soon
after childbirth. She and her husband have come to take many luxuries
as basic necessities, and they are hesitant to do without.

When a woman's income constitutes half or more of the family resources, then staying home to raise a child becomes the luxury that can be passed on. Of course, high-priced aspirations for their offspring, such as summer camp, private schools, and the like, only increase their expenses. The impulse to return to work cannot be easily resisted.

Finally, because she is well educated and cosmopolitan, a modern Jewish woman is likely to hold liberal opinions regarding birth control. More so and for the same reasons, she is probably adept at translating these attitudes into behavior. One study comparing white, married women of different faiths between the ages of 18 and 44 confirms this fact graphically.

The data revealed that 73 percent of Catholic and 79 percent of Protestant respondents said that they used some form of birth control. By contrast, the figure was 91 percent for Jewish respondents. It might be added that because of her training and professional orientations, the Jewish woman is also probably more successful in applying these methods, thereby rendering them more effective.

The sum of these overlapping forces leaves at least one unmistakable conclusion. The young, professional Jewish woman of whom we speak will have fewer children than did her mother. Indeed she will probably have fewer than she herself had originally anticipated.

Surely this is all true of non-Jewish women as well. Sociologists and demographers have said as much. They have noted that, not surprisingly, the trend seems to increase in direct proportion to the education, profession, and affluence of the woman in question. Because Jewish women tend to be better educated, more upwardly mobile, employed in more professional positions, and from more affluent families than their gentile sisters, these trends are yet more acute among Jewish women.

IV

One further set of challenges emerges at the opposite end of the demographic scale, relating to the growing proportion of elderly people in the U.S. Jewish population. It too can be understood as a result of the great affluence that has accrued to U.S. Jews.

There are several ways to document the trend. For example, data gathered over the past ten years suggest that the median age for Jews in this country is approximately 36 years. In the city of New York, wherein reside about one-third of U.S. Jews, the median age is almost 40.

This sets them apart as the oldest ethnic group in the United States. By contrast, the median age for the general white population is 29, for blacks it is 26, and for Hispanics, the youngest of the ethnic groups, the median age is 23. To be sure, a falling birth rate contributes to this phenomenon as the younger cohorts become an increasingly smaller part of the population. But affluence also contributes to the tendency for Jews to live longer and healthier lives than they did before, and longer than do their gentile neighbors.

It is no revelation that people who can best afford it are most likely to have appropriate medical care. Among their earliest priorities will be proper health insurance, with coverage through their employment or based on their personal abilities to pay. Indeed for many, health and medical benefits are evaluated as an integral part of the compensation package.

Those of upper socioeconomic status are also more likely to have a personal physician, unlike the common practice among the poor to depend upon the emergency room of a local hospital for primary care. In addition, they are more likely to visit their physician in advance of a crisis and to follow medical instructions despite cost and inconvenience.

The most common medical needs—childbirth, well care, routine surgery, as well as hospitalization and medication—are more likely to get timely and appropriate attention, at standards that equal or exceed requirements. Basic sanitation, nutrition, and shelter will not be a difficulty. Consequently, the more flagrant examples of negligence and lack of proper care that tend to shorten the life expectancies of Americans do not have quite the same sting within the Jewish community.

The effects are still more graphic when viewed somewhat indirectly. Over the past ten to fifteen years there has been a dramatic shift in Jewish residential patterns that epitomizes Jewish longevity. In the decade ending in 1980, for example, the city of New York lost roughly one third of its Jewish population. By contrast, the Jewish population of Miami Beach increased by about 60 percent.

Certainly, part of this change relates to the general exodus from the big cities that took place during this period. It also reflects a personal as well as corporate rush to the Sun Belt that robbed many urban centers of their tax base and middle-class foundation. But there can be no denying that the shift clearly denotes an aging Jewish population, moving from adult homesteads toward retirement villages.

Once again, the social and economic success of the Jewish community in the United States has contributed to the physical well-being of its members and to their life expectancies. It is not that they are living longer just because they are Jewish. They are living longer because they have the wherewithal to promote their own health and prevent fatality even in the event of accident and disease. Their affluence and education, in turn, are clearly related to their ethnic and religious identifications.

In many ways these findings imply more a blessing than a challenge. Long life is an indication of successful living by any definition. Moreover, it is evidence of not just individual but also group success.

Personal health is generally related to a system of effective familial support and communal response, as well as to cultural and educational heritage. It indicates that appropriate services are part of the community, that its members utilize them, and that they are working. Put succinctly, physical longevity denotes social and cultural longevity as well. It also suggests an individual and communal disdain for recklessness, violence, and abuse that are frequently the cause of suicide, accidental death, and high rates of morbidity elsewhere. This may be functional as well as traditional, and it may be couched in religious or social terms.

To be part of a complex social and familial system is to value one's life and the lives of those closest. It is also to recognize and to renew transcendent commitments to family and friends, despite powerful temptations to the contrary. Put simply, it gives reason to live and live in a healthy manner and to resist momentary gratification.

The aging trend also meets many Jewish values. As with most traditional cultures, Judaism venerates elders, extending to them respect both for their years and for the wisdom they have presumably accrued. Children have broad responsibilities toward their parents and must always accord them a deferential status. Indeed, the Bible offers long life to those who are fastidious in the requirement to honor their parents.

But the aging trend has also brought with it a series of difficulties that are more the outgrowth of the quality of life than the number of its years. As before, these are issues that emerge from the integration of the Jewish community and its success within U.S. society. One aspect has to do with income distribution in the Jewish community along generational lines. Indeed there are many older Jews who live comfortably and whose needs are cared for, and, as we have argued, it was a higher standard of living and of health care that contributed toward their longevity.

But upward mobility, particularly over the past twenty years, has meant outward mobility, as well. Extended families have been divided as children have married and moved away from the old neighborhoods. Grandparents' contacts with their grandchildren have been limited to occasional visits because their children have moved to suburban communities in all parts of the country and because they have sought retirement homes themselves.

That hasn't been true for all, however. Particularly in the big cities of the North, there is a disproportionate number of elderly Jews among the poor. Many have remained in their old neighborhoods, resisting the suburban exodus that carried away their children and grandchildren in the past two decades. Some refused to leave their friends, their local synagogues, and the community they loved. Others simply couldn't affort to move.

While they did not move, their neighborhoods did. The familiar faces were replaced by those with strange names, cultures, and ethnic identities. In many cases, the remaining few have become prey to local bullies, addicts, and street gangs. Afraid to leave their apartments to shop or simply to stroll, they have become hostages in their homes.

The irony is that many have families not an hour's drive from the old neighborhoods. Some offspring are too busy or taken with their own lives to invite an elder parent to join them. More than a few complain that they have begged Mama and Papa to move away, but the latter have refused. How can they leave their apartment of thirty years—even if it has become a bunker in the urban wars?

By contrast, the aging trend also raises important challenges for the children of the elderly. While there is universal concern for the question of physical well-being, there is something ironic in the way elder care emerges for children approaching retirement themselves.

Picture a couple that have worked hard all their lives. They have raised a family successfully. Their youngest is either married himself or completing his professional education, that is, he is "well on his way.'' Completing their familial responsibilities, they look forward to a well-deserved and comfortable retirement.

But alas, Mama and Papa, now over eighty, need help. Barely able to fend for themselves, it is clear that some arrangement will have to be made to see to their care. Do we make room for one or two more and delay retirement? Do we engage the services of a full-time companion or aide to allow them to remain in the old apartment? Do we put an elderly parent in a home? For many, the decision is fraught with guilt.

Others have been all too callous in seeking its resolution. Sadly, there have been those who have exploited the guilt. Nursing homes, day programs, skilled-care facilities, and home-care agencies have popped up in the most unlikely places. Many are operated by people who have little or no experience and whose primary motives are profit oriented. The scandals that have become legion in long-term care stand as painful testament to the entire affair.

V

The message is clear. U.S. Jews have reached a level of success far beyond anything conjured in the minds of the simple immigrants who were their forebears. On measures of affluence, education, and occupational status, they outstrip virtually every other ethnic group in this country.

Moreover, their influence is felt beyond the bounds of the community. It is telling, for example, that of twelve immigrants honored for their contribution to American life at the recent rededication of the Statue of Liberty, five were born Jewish. Their success on these shores has never been parochial. It reaches well into the culture that is their host.

With these impressive credentials have come important challenges as well. As they have climbed the social and economic ladder, they have undergone important demographic changes that affect not only numbers, they influence the very structure of the community in the United States.

Families have shrunk, birth rates have fallen, and our youth marry later and at substantially different stations then did their parents. Their affiliations—indeed their choice to make any affiliation—have been realigned in short order. Their general willingness to support communal needs with their time and resources has dwindled and shifted with them.

In it all, we see the influence of female assertiveness, which seems to have had a more intensive impact upon the Jewish community than upon the population as a whole. Because they are a metropolitan community and because their women are better educated, more affluent, and more upwardly mobile, they are more likely to hold professional and managerial positions that make powerful demands upon their time and energies.

Consequently, they are willing to devote less of themselves to child rearing and traditional family activities and often choose surrogates to fill these roles. In addition, they have sought to shrink the extent and duration of these responsibilities to the point that it has been reflected in the demographic patterns already listed.

By the same token, Jews are a rapidly aging community, perhaps the oldest in the United States. Many activists are graduating from years of involvement in community affairs. We can expect a crisis of leadership—quantitative and qualitative—in the immediate future. There will be fewer lay people available to take their places, and those who are available may not be so easily given to volunteerism.

In addition, there has been an association between aging and low income within the Jewish community. There are many who stand in need of support. However, their visibility is limited by the absence of effective advocacy and by the fact that they represent a small proportion of Jews. Important changes are required to protect the gains won on the socioeconomic battlefields of the United States.

Perhaps it is simply a matter of communication. If raising children is a communal priority in Jewish life, then it must be reinstated among those values that parents normally impart to their children. The importance and the impact of family life has always been a vital aspect of Jewish culture. It has been a value passed on to succeeding generations by word and deed, as much through formal training as by example.

It is only recently that parents have avoided such discussions or have relegated them to secondary status in favor of encouraging academic, professional, and material success. Aspirations of marriage and children should be as natural an element of upbringing as university attendance or professional education. The two must not be perceived as mutually exclusive.

This is not to suggest that females must be superwomen, having jobs, children, homemaking responsibilities, and more. Doing it all doesn't mean having it all. Those who have attempted it have found it to be anything but liberating.

Nor is it to suggest that young men are absolved of responsibility in this demographic challenge to traditional Jewish values. After all, if many Jewish women are marrying later, so are many Jewish men. The realities of Western culture, however, dictate that men approaching middle age may marry women ten to twenty years their junior. Fate, cruel as it often is, has not dealt women an equal hand here.

And if Jewish family values are to survive, then men will also have to rethink their commitments of time and resource to family and children, commitments that so often pale in favor of their predominant role as breadwinner. Well-educated and professionally trained women will not simply cast aside their values and aspirations to immerse themselves in motherhood. Moreover, an upscale lifestyle demands the benefits of two professional incomes. Husbands will have to serve as full partners in the familial enterprise, sharing even its least rewarding tasks just as they share their wife's salary.

It is simply to suggest that family responsibilities be regarded as equal to those of education and profession. It is not only the latter that lead to success and satisfaction. Indeed, even secular feminists have recently reconsidered some of their more radical pronouncements. They have allowed that there are redeeming virtues in family life without which professional accomplishment may be hollow and incomplete. One who raises children effectively makes a statement equal to that of one who delivers them.

The issues raise important questions for U.S. society in general. One is not quite sure what will result from a generation that has been raised in smaller families under the tutelage of various forms of day care and surrogate parenting. Nor is it clear how well our society will respond to the growing numbers and proportions of aged in its midst. For the Jewish community, however, the issues are nothing less than crucial.

2

Out of the Faith

I

I looked up at the stylish middle-aged lady who entered my small office. She was a member of the executive board and I recognized her immediately. I rose quickly to clear a place for her to sit. Each chair was piled high with books and papers. During my several months on the job, there had been few visitors to this cubicle with no windows that passed for my office.

As director of the Jewish education in this large women's organization, it was generally my job to attend meetings and visit volunteer leaders at their offices or in the grand conference rooms on the third floor. Rarely did one of them venture up here. Her presence was already causing a bit of a stir outside my door. I chose to ignore the whispers.

Somehow this was different, though. I could see immediately that my guest was not here on organizational business. Her furrowed brow suggested something more personal, something very troubling.

She motioned for me to sit down as she found a place for herself among the files, the folders, and the mess. She was impeccably tailored and quite youthful. But I guessed that the golden tresses were not natural, and the thin lines at her eyes revealed a more accurate estimation of her years with the organization.

She smiled nervously and began one of the more bizarre conversations of my professional life. "I'm very impressed with the work you're doing as director of Jewish education," she began, sort of greasing the wheels for the real issue at hand. "And I want you to know that others have taken notice as well," she smiled again. "Why, we were just talking about you at our executive meeting this morning."

"You're very kind," I said, sensing that there was more behind this off-chance meeting. She went on, almost without hearing me.

"And I guess that's why I've chosen to talk with you." She shifted in her chair. "You see, I'm hoping that you can offer me some direction about a dilemma my family is facing. It's really rather personal," she said, a nervous cough overtaking her. She composed herself in short order. "So I'm hoping that I can depend upon your discretion. . . ."

I looked at her, puzzled. "Of course," I said, "you can count on me, in any way that I can help."

"Good," she said. "By the way, I understand that you're also a rabbi." She offered it in the form of a question, but I sensed that she already knew the answer.

"Yes," I replied, "I am ordained, but I don't practice—that is, I don't hold a pulpit." What's she driving at anyway? I wondered.

"Well here it is, Rabbi" she smiled, putting special emphasis on the last word. "My daughter is a junior at an excellent college, out of state, you know. And she's just returned for the Thanksgiving recess. And," she said proudly, "she's found herself a fine young man."

"Marvelous!" I said almost instinctively. "Mazel tov, congratulations! This is wonderful news." Now it begins to fit together, I mused. She's probably going to ask me to officiate at the wedding.

"Yes," she said, responding to my good wishes. "Thank you. We're very happy. But there is one thing." Red lights went off in my mind. No, I thought, not an executive board member.

"You see," she went on, "Tim is not Jewish. He comes from a fine Presbyterian family in Connecticut." What a pain. I hope she's not going to ask me to officiate with their minister or something.

"Well," she said slowly, "we had a heck of a time finding a rabbi who would marry them. You know, the kids really don't care if we have one or not." She smiled patronizingly. "But we all thought that since Tim's pastor would be there . . . " There was a brief pause. I sat motionless. "These rabbis are so sticky about these things," she said almost angrily. "It's really barbaric. I mean, this is the twentieth century."

She raised her hands for emphasis. "We've belonged to that darn temple for almost thirty years, and when we asked our rabbi to officiate, he wouldn't hear of it. We'll probably cancel our membership when this is over." Some nerve, that rabbi. He actually has integrity.

"But that's neither here nor there," she went on, interrupting my musings. "Anyway, we found a young rabbi who agreed to perform the ceremony with Reverend Mitchell."

"That's wonderful," I said slowly, only half sardonically. More than anything, I was relieved for not having been asked to get involved. "Everything sounds like it's working out fine."

"Well, there's still a problem," she said, wrinkling her brow once more. "You see, the rabbi we found, Rabbi Carlton, well, he's a fine young man and all. We've met him and we're all very impressed."

She took a deep breath and collected her thoughts. "My problem is this," she began slowly. "You see, Rabbi Carlton belongs to Breira, you know that terrible left-wing organization that wants to force some sort of dovish peace plan on the Israeli government. It really bothers me, I mean, how would it look, a member of the executive board of our organization. . . . "

Her words hit me like clumps of concrete. I stared at her for a moment. It's his politics that worry her, for Pete's sake. My face must have shown the incredulous passions I felt.

"Well," she stammered, "I thought that maybe you as a rabbi and an educator yourself, maybe you could give me some guidance. I mean, I really want to do what's best for everybody, and I don't want to cause any unnecessary problems here. Still," she said with newfound vigor, "I do have my values!"

"Let me understand," I said slowly, still not quite sure I had heard her correctly. "Your daughter is marrying a fellow named Tim, whose Protestant parents come from Connecticut." She nodded. "And that's not a problem for you, I mean the fact that he's not Jewish."

"Oh no," she said with that same patronizing smile. "My husband and I discussed it and that's never been an issue at all. We're really quite beyond that sort of thing."

I went on, choosing to ignore her response, hoping that she wasn't going to tell me that it was the twentieth century again. "And you're asking me if you should be concerned with the rabbi's preference for a dovish position on the Middle East . . . "

"Well, yes," she said again, "I do have my values."

II

In the very short space of a generation, intermarriage has become such a common occurence in the Jewish community that it is easily taken for granted. At the least, it is no longer a shock; indeed, in many circles it is more chic than shock. In this development lies one of the most profound challenges to Jewish survival that our long and motley history has ever sustained.

Elsewhere we have discussed the effect of falling birth rates and a rapidly aging population. Alongside both phenomena, intermarriage serves as one more contributory factor to the decline of our numbers in this country and elsewhere, and it goes far in restructuring the community that will remain.

Even a cursory glance at the data can be startling. Over the past thirty years, there has been a dramatic increase in the numbers and in the proportion of Jews choosing to marry Gentiles. The geometric proportions by which the trend has increased has turned an isolated instance into a commonplace.

For example, though somewhat sketchy, early data suggest that prior to 1957, intermarriage rates, that is, the proportion of Jews marrying Gentiles in which no conversion occurs before the marriage, were fairly stable at about 10 percent. By the mid-1960s, however, the rate jumped to over 17 percent, a substantial increase in only a few years.*

The events of the next decades were still more dramatic. Within ten years, the rate of intermarriage almost doubled—to approximately 32 percent. Though estimates vary, it is reasonable to assume that today about 40 percent of Jews who marry do not choose Jewish partners.

In addition, there are some interesting inferences to be made from the backgrounds of Jews who intermarry. About 11 percent come from

*Most of the data presented here are based on a series of studies conducted by Egon Mayer under the auspices of the American Jewish Committee. See, for example, Egon Mayer and Carl Shengold, *Intermarriage and the Jewish Future* (New York: American Jewish Committee, 1979) and Egon Mayer, *Love and Tradition: Marriage Between Jews and Christians* (New York: Plenum, 1985).

families of Orthodox affiliation; over 29 percent come from Conservative families; 27 percent are from Reform families; and 33 percent are
from unaffiliated families. Ironically, these are roughly the proportions
of such affiliations in the U.S. Jewish community as a whole, with
something of an underrepresentation of the unaffiliated.

In other words, the data suggest that Jews of various denominations
(or no domination at all) are intermarrying at about their rate in the
population, that is, what we would expect of them randomly. Whether
their parents belonged to one group or another doesn't make much
difference. Religious structures of one form or another do not seem to
prevent intermarriage, nor does their absence encourage it. From the
Orthodox to the unaffiliated, intermarriage is intermarriage.

We also know a good deal about the kinds of Jews who choose to
marry out of their faith. The substantial majority are Jewish males,
although among younger respondents, the sexual proportions are closer.
Most intermarried Jews have had a Hebrew education of some sort, at
least through their bar or bat mitzvah.

The majority come from homes that either did not own or did not
use Sabbath candles, a Kiddush cup, *tallith* and *tefillin* (Jewish ritual
objects used in prayer), a Passover seder plate, a Jewish Bible, or
prayer books. Ironically, the most popular ritual object in their homes
was the menorah, the Hanukkah lamp. Though a relatively minor fes-
tival, Hanukkah has prospered for its serendipitous calendar position,
parallel to Christmas. In most cases, it has been redefined as the Jewish contribution to the holiday season.

By contrast, the majority of non-Jewish partners were Protestants
whose parents were less unfavorably disposed to the idea of intermarriage than were their Jewish counterparts. In addition, about one in
five non-Jewish spouses convert to Judaism (generally the female),
while virtually none of the Jewish partners convert to the faith of their
spouses.

The mention of conversion introduces one of the most intriguing of
all findings; it also suggests an important pathway for the future. As
noted, in a minority of cases, the gentile partner does convert, whether
from genuine commitment to Jewish ritual and community or for reasons of marriage and family unity. When that occurs, for whatever
reason, there is a sharp increase in Jewish affiliation and ritual observance on the part of both partners. In fact, the increase even overtakes

the general religious practices of endogamous families, that is, similar families in which both partners are born Jewish. The data are illuminating.

For example, fewer than 20 percent of intermarried couples in which no conversion occurs later affiliate with a synagogue. By contrast, the figure for couples in which the gentile partner converts is almost 70 percent. In fact, synagogue affiliation for the general U.S. Jewish population is only about 60 percent.

Synagogue attendance tells the same story. Some 40 percent of Jews married to non-Jews who did not convert said that they never attended High Holy Day services. Attendance in the general Jewish population is not much better. A survey of Jews in the New York metropolitan area, for example, found that 30 percent never attended religious services of any type.

But here's the kicker. For intermarried couples in which the gentile partner converted, the figure of those attending no religious services drops to only about 10 percent. It is not surprising, therefore, that in a majority of their homes they own, use, or display Sabbath candles, a Jewish prayer book, and other Jewish books.

The implications are clear. From a purely sociological and demographic perspective, it makes good sense to pursue conversion of the non-Jewish partner to an intermarriage. Theological considerations aside, the conclusion holds even if the conversion is undertaken purely as a matter of convenience at the time and for no other reason than for the marriage itself.

III

A few editorial observations are in order. There are some who, while not necessarily questioning the data, do question the concern being raised here. On the contrary, they argue, over the long haul intermarriage may be to our advantage. It can be made to support the survival of the Jewish community as a minority enclave in a sea of gentiles.

By reaching out, by joining with our hosts in marriage and family life, we expand outward the locus of support for Jewish causes and for the Jewish community. Through this ultimate form of integration, we forge bonds with some who might not otherwise be so well disposed on our behalf. In regard to the entire agenda of Jewish issues— Israel, anti-Semitism, Jewish education, philanthropy, and communal welfare—intermarriage extends our circle of friends, allies, and affili-ates. It quintessentially culminates our American Jewish ethos.

Anyway, they conclude, it's no longer a matter for debate. It's sim-ply a fact of life, a given, a part of the price we pay for mobility and affluence in this "golden land." Instead of wringing our hands and pounding our fists, it behooves us to reach out to these people and their families, to legitimate their presence in our midst, and to include them—and their children, particularly—within the bounds of our com-munal family.

As if to underscore the argument, the Reform movement has re-cently formalized a long-standing and highly controversial practice. Its rabbis have chosen to accept the children of intermarriage as fully credentialed members of the community, with or without the benefit of conversion, no matter which of their parents were born Jewish. The move has raised a furor among more traditional elements of U.S. Jewry, where classical usage defines religious status solely by the heredity of the mother.

No doubt this new/old position was informed by some of the argu-ments noted above. And no doubt its underpinnings include a de facto recognition that this has been unofficial practice within the Reform movement for over fifty years. In any event, they reason, their con-versions are not generally recognized by more conservative Jewish re-ligious leadership in the United States or Israel, so they see no loss in making it official.

Their rationale aside, however, the data at hand simply do not bear out such sanguine suppositions. To be sure, there appears to be a gen-eral reduction of the more classic forms of anti–Semitism in this coun-try. There is also broad and increasing support for Israel's survival. But by no stretch of the imagination could much of that be remotely attributed to the products of intermarriage.

On the contrary, children of intermarried families tend to estrange and isolate themselves from organized Jewish life, even more so than their cohorts in the general Jewish community. In fact, only one in four even identify themselves as Jews, and only about one in ten say that ethnic ties are very important for them. Apparently, it's less for lack of outreach than for lack of their interest that they are little in-volved.

Their disinterest is well rooted. The majority of their males have not undergone ritual circumcision (Brith Milah) nor have most of them, male or female, been afforded a bar or bat mitzvah. Some three out of four of them have had no formal Jewish education whatsoever. Rather than promoting Jewish awareness in a broader public, intermarriage hastens still further the tendency toward its dissolution.

In no small degree the attraction between Jews and non-Jews that appears to have exploded in recent years may be related to an interesting set of stereotypes on both sides of the aisle. Here there is little formal data and a good deal of the thinking is impressionistic, almost intuitive. But the results are potent.

On the one hand rabbinic counselors and interested observers, particularly at university campuses, have noted an interesting phenomenon among gentile women contemplating intermarriage. Of course all declare their love and devotion for their intended, a commitment that will transcend any differences in their backgrounds or in their outlook. Most profess little taste for the religious affiliations of their birth, anyway.

But a good many add a fascinating insight. Apparently, they have been reared with the idea that Jewish men make good husbands, maybe the best. They are less likely to abuse their wives or children, they are less likely to drink, and they have a strong commitment to family life. By contrast, they are more likely to be well educated and come from affluent families with traditional values. The sum, therefore, is that they will provide well for their wives and children.

Perhaps there is substantial truth in mother's wisdom. Yet, whether they are accurate or erroneous, and whether they are taken seriously at the conscious level or simply dismissed as wild imaginings, may be beside the point. At some profound level these stereotypes take hold. They influence, however unconsciously, even decisions of such moment as the choice of a mate. While they are difficult to measure, to document, and to define, that doesn't make them absent.

The stereotype has its opposite number within the Jewish community. For over a generation, this country's literary lions—with Jewish novelists, playwrights, and screen writers at their head—have reinforced a negative popular attitude toward Jewish women.

From Mrs. Portnoy we learn that Jewish mothers are pushy, demanding, and emasculating. They leave little room for their husbands and sons to grow, to express themselves, indeed to be themselves. Instead, they cover dissension with a mound of heavy food that is underspiced and poorly cooked. And they are, after all, role models for their daughters.

Speaking of whom, at the opposite end of the buffet, we have been fed images of bitchy, pampered young women who give very little but ask for the world. From Private Benjamin we learn that Jewish girls are spoiled and demanding creatures. They have been pampered all their lives, and their every wish is Papa's lifelong command.

The mirror holds a very unflattering reflection. Jewish sons have been raised by overbearing mothers. For all their intellect and education, these men have no minds of their own. They are weak willed and lack self-direction. In the vernacular, they are wimps and nerds.

Jewish daughters, by contrast, can never be satisfied materially. The luxuries that others dream about are only commonplace for Daddy's little princess. They show little appreciation for their husband's efforts, and soon enough, they become Jewish mothers themselves.

Perhaps this denigration of the Jewish female is matched with the stereotypical beliefs about the quality of Jewish husbands held by many in non-Jewish circles. If so, it helps explain, at least in part, why Jewish men are more likely to intermarry than are their sisters.

In either case, these are not the social or sexual images one normally conjures in his or her search for a marital partner. While it may not be possible to statistically associate any of these stereotypes to intermarriage rates directly, they can't help but aggravate already acute conditions.

It all comes together about the time these young folks, male and female, Jewish and gentile, go away to school. For many non-Jews, this is the first time that they will meet Jewish classmates and colleagues in any number. At a residential institution, particularly, the encounter will be much more intense than any they have had before. Given the disproportionate numbers of Jews who are students, faculty, and staff at America's numerous campuses, the opportunities will be manifold.

The same is probably true for most of the Jewish students. They will be far from parental supervision and traditional moorings for the first time in their lives. The free and open atmosphere fostered at a university and the penchant for experimentation that is its hallmark make this situation most conducive to developing new and perhaps erstwhile forbidden relationships.

Those concerned with intermarriage might justifiably conclude that it behooves good Jewish parents to see to it that their kids don't dorm out of town. But for the bulk of U.S. Jews the mere suggestion is absurd. People marked by a passion for education, mobility, and professional success, as are most within the Jewish community, will not prevent their children from attending any school or university, nor will they limit their educational and professional opportunities in other ways. But short of that, perhaps one small recommendation is in order.

It is considered fine style to investigate the quality of a university's premedical program. It is acceptable to ask about the law school placement record of a given college. Its athletic programs, housing facilities, dining plan, and certainly its tuition rates are all traditional stops along the route that ultimately leads to the choice of a school.

Why, then, is it not acceptable, trendy, or chic to inquire after the quality of Jewish life on a given campus? The details are simple and straightforward. Are there many Jewish kids on campus? Do they have a center, an organization, a program? Are there social and academic activities for them?

Similarly, is there a local community or professional agency to support and channel their interests? Is there a formal or informal program of instruction available should they be inclined to further their Jewish education even as they pursue their professional training? Ought these not be included as reasonable criteria in the choice of a university? One senses that, generally, they are not.

IV

"Professor, this is really one of the most uncomfortable moments of my life." The voice at the other end of the phone was sweet and sincere, but firm. Clearly, the young lady to whom it belonged was schooled in all the social graces, but it was just as clear that she had a mind of her own. And it had been set, long before I accepted this patently absurd assignment.

"Just talk to her," her mother had asked me, "please. Maybe you can reach her." Here was this wonderful former student of mine whom I now considered a friend, a woman in her late middle years, successful by any definition, yet facing one of the most difficult confrontations of her adult life.

She had raised three children in classic secular style. They each attended the finest schools, camps, and enrichment programs available and their parents invested everything in them. That's why this all was a shock and a puzzlement to her. Still she was willing to reason. Her husband, on the other hand, would hear nothing of it at all.

It seems that their eldest, a graduate of one of this country's premier universities and professional schools, had been living for several years with a gentile classmate, a child of local Catholic upbringing. This was blow enough.

But now the young couple wanted to formalize their feelings for one another in a marriage ceremony, and they were calling upon their parents to bless the union. I never found out what his parents thought of it all. But my friend requested that I try to dissuade her daughter over the phone.

If all else failed, she told me to tell her daughter in no uncertain terms that it would "kill her father."

"Why," I asked this sophisticated young woman whom I never would meet, "why have you decided to marry? After all, you've been living together for about three years, and it seems to have worked out all right." Never had I imagined that I one day would be supporting cohabitation over marriage.

"Well," she said slowly, "I guess we just weren't ready to take the plunge before. But now that we've both completed law school, and we've had a few years to really get to know each other, well . . . I don't know, I guess now we're ready."

"You know how your parents feel about the decision."

"Well," she said, a bit flustered for the first time. "Actually, I never expected that they would react this way. I mean, they knew that we were living together. They even met Robert when they visited last year." I could hear her fiancé whispering something in the background. The words were muffled. He seemed to be trying to comfort her, trying to get her to change the subject, but she paid him no mind. "Really," she went on, her pace picking up a bit, "all my life I've been encouraged to mix and mingle with all types of people. I mean, my family isn't religious at all. We never attended *shul* much. And we certainly weren't kosher."

She laughed sharply, maybe too sharply. "My parents took us to Chinese restaurants every Sunday, when we were kids. And we almost never celebrated the holidays or anything." She paused. Her mind seemed to wander for a second.

When she returned, it was as if she wanted to justify herself. "We were always taught that being Jewish means being ethical, you know, doing the right things, being honest and like that. Really, I can't understand why my parents are taking it like this."

I had heard the story before. Parents raise their children in a secular environment, liberated and enlightened. They rarely express the differences in their culture or heritage and accept their liberalism as a form of secular religion. Why should they be surprised when their children take that upbringing to its logical conclusion?

Their reaction when the inevitable occurs is to seek out some poor rabbi and dump it all in his lap. Now this fellow has to confront the happy young couple. He barely remembers the Jewish partner for all the contact he's had with the family over the years, yet he's expected to turn it around with a phone call or an hour's conference.

Of course there's no way that he can succeed. For the most part, the kids are only there as a favor. It's little more than a ritual for them, a rite of passage that they endure so that they can get on with the show.

When the rabbi fails, as circumstances dictate that he must, the whole damn thing becomes his fault. "After all," the parents will tell their sympathetic friends, self-righteously, "didn't we take them to the rabbi!"

But I'm being too rough here. Her mother came to me seeking support, not anger and cynicism. Still, what do you say under the circumstances—mazel tov?

The kids are likeable, attractive, and intelligent, but they are not going to be convinced by all the traditional arguments. It's useless at this point to talk about how the survival of the Jewish people depends upon their marital decisions or how the losses of the Holocaust must be replaced by families and children born within the faith.

They're walking away from a faith that their ancestors died for. But you can't walk away from something that you don't have. The time to inculcate some sense of Jewish history and purpose was about twenty years ago.

She interrupted my thoughts. "The way my father is acting, I think, is the most disturbing of all." I had been told that she was always very close to him, that she valued their relationship and wouldn't want to hurt him.

"You see, he doesn't really care that I'm marrying a Catholic. All he's asking for is some sort of conversion. Really, any sort, by any rabbi would do. You know, wave a magic wand and poof! you're converted. Just so that he could say that his new son-in-law was Jewish.''

We talked about the implications of a conversion and the reasons why parents who never showed much interest in Jewish life might now take a do-or-die position. Her father made it clear that if she went through with the marriage he would not attend the wedding. He also threatened to sever their relationship in the future. I sensed that the more firm was his stance, the more resolute was his daughter.

"Here," she said finally, "my fiancé would like to talk." So I would speak with the mysterious young man, her paramour and the object of all this passion and angst.

I found him to be a pleasant fellow, moderately intelligent, calm, and friendly. He was certainly not the epitome of evil that had probably been conjured in the minds of his unwilling in-laws-to-be. Actually, I kind of liked him. What's more, he seemed genuinely interested in the process of conversion and the philosophy behind it. Already, my mind began to work. Hey! I might be able to pull this one out yet, with some encouragement, maybe.

"Wait a minute, babe," his sweetheart interrupted our talk on the other extension. "We discussed this," she said to him firmly, "and I thought we agreed that we weren't going to let anyone else make our decisions. A meaningless ritual like this, just for my father's benefit— it's only going to become an obstacle for us later. It'll stand between us, you know—something major that you had to do for me."

Fool that I was. For a brief moment I had allowed my naive optimism to get the better of me. We talked a bit more, but I wasn't even convincing myself. I invited them to explore the options further, to visit with me, have dinner perhaps. But they politely declined, as I knew they would.

I hung up with a heavy heart. It wasn't that I expected to succeed. Actually, I could simply say good riddance and put it all out of my mind, but I knew the cost of failure. These were some of our best and our brightest, and we really need all the talent we can get.

The chances of this couple retaining a link with the Jewish community are small indeed. As for their children, the chances are even smaller. This wasn't a personal failure. It was worse. It was a communal failure. In the long run, I sensed that I would suffer for it—as part of that community.

3

Orthodoxy Resurgent

I

The European Jew arrived on these shores at the turn of the century with high expectations. Gold lay in the streets, he believed, and diamonds hung from the branches of every tree. No more the oppressive political system that prevented mobility from without. No more the poverty and illiteracy of the shtetl, the hamlet in which he was born. He would never return to its harsh social system, which prevented his mobility from within. This was a new world with open values.

His optimism was reinforced by every cousin, uncle, and brother-in-law who had made the journey first. No matter that they met with little of the expected success, that their living conditions were little improved over what they left behind. No matter that they lacked even the small bit of status and the very large bit of security that the *shtetl* did afford. They certainly were not about to admit that to their green-horn relatives who would only chorus, "I told you so." Instead, they wrote of the glories of the *goldeneh medinah*, this golden land. After all, appearances are also important. So convincing were their letters that they spawned still further immigration. Everyone seemed to have a rich cousin in America.

The new arrival was prepared to accommodate himself to his adopted environment. A new world required a new name, new clothes, a new

This chapter is an expanded and updated version of "Orthodoxy Resurgent," originally published in *Judaism*, Fall 1981.

language, and, most important of all, a new outlook. The old ways were perhaps functional in Europe. Anyway, there wasn't much choice back there. But not here, not in America! Here one had to be a ''yenkey.'' The beard, the long black coat, the sidelocks—thay all had to go. Kosher food was terribly expensive and not always available. Working on the Sabbath was usually not a matter of choice. And how better to insure the successful assimilation of one's children than to see that their rearing and their education were laced with American values?

In this way, the Jewish immigrant was much like those of other persuasions, only more so. America has always been a largely secular and pragmatic affair. It is still much imbued with the ideology of the melting pot. At best, strict religious observance, imported from the old country, is an obstacle. It may be tolerable in the first generation, but discouraged thereafter. At worst, it is suspect.

Most Jewish immigrants embraced these secular values with a religious passion. In response, American Jewish theology, and the institutions created in its support, sought to recognize, even legitimate, assimilationist impulses within the context of the faith. It was the American way.

For a previous generation of immigrants, the tenets of Reform Judaism appeared most appropriate. The movement had been relatively unsuccessful in Central Europe during the early and mid-nineteenth century. Its thinking was too radical; the more conservative religious establishment was too well entrenched. By contrast, those who chose to loose their bonds with the Jewish community in Europe simply converted.

But the United States was different. Here Reform found fertile ground among early Jewish communities where formally trained rabbinic personnel of any persuasion were few and far between. Notably, German-Jewish immigrants saw its theology as a reasonable compromise with their new environment and their steady rise after the Civil War.

So aspiration and ritual met, both structurally and theologically. Temples were built on the order of high church, with segregation of the sexes eliminated and organ recitals introduced. Beliefs and practices that inhibited involvement in the best that secular society could offer were dropped officially. They had long since been dropped by most congregants anyway.

Even the word *Jew* was considered in poor taste, pejorative and demeaning. It was frequently replaced by the softer, more classical *Hebrew* in the names of institutions and in personal identification, hence the Hebrew Union College or the Union of American Hebrew Congregations. More than anything else, these new Americans were concerned with their acceptance by gentile countrymen. They sought to protect their fragile status here. This goes far in explaining their shock at individual manifestations of official anti-Semitism, for example, Grant's limitations on Jewish trade in the Union army camps or specific restrictions on Jewish travelers in one or another resort. That Jews had been mistreated in Europe for centuries was well known, but the United States was supposed to be different.

It also explains much of their initial rejection of Zionism. Attempts to rebuild a Jewish homeland were threatening on both social and theological grounds. In the words of one U.S. Reform rabbi of the late nineteenth century: "This country is our Palestine, this city our Jerusalem."

II

But the newer arrivals from Eastern Europe, always more pious and less socially aware, were not quite prepared to go that far, at least not at first. Probably more from social discomfort than theological commitment, they could not attend the grand services at Reform temples, nor were they encouraged to do so. Neither could they afford the social amenities associated with it, if indeed such were their aspirations. They were, after all, poor cousins. They would be cared for by their wealthier brethren, if only they would stay downtown, quiet and deferentially out of sight. Conflicts between these "Ostjuden" (as the East Europeans were derisively called) and the "Yahudim" or "Yankel Doodles" (as they called their uptown coreligionists) were legion and were immortalized in legend, stage, and song.

The circumstances soon served as a catalyst to the birth of yet another theological form. Its raison d'être would be compromise; its structure, pluralist; and its direction, lay. To be sure, there would be accommodations with a new environment, but they would take place with loyalty to the faith.

This might be a middle ground for the new immigrants and particularly for their children, most of whom still felt an abiding tie to the

"God of their fathers" but who had been raised in the U.S. milieu.
As its name implies, this uniquely American religious form would be
genuinely conservative in its approach as it sought to make peace with
the New World.

The sensibilities of its founders notwithstanding, traditionalism, piety
and strict observance were soon left behind. At most they were relegated to the older and poorer classes as the bulk of its adherents rushed
headlong toward the American dream. Following the organizational
imperative, large, powerful, and fairly cohesive units were created or
extended to serve as the lay, communal, and rabbinic arms of U.S.
Jewry's more liberal branches.

As these replaced the primitive initial structures, liberal values became increasingly institutionalized, soon insinuating their way into
doctrine. It all began in the search for a religious medium marked by
flexibility and change, but it soon became a full-blown theology driven,
in practice, more by its periphery than by its center.

Everything to the theological right of these new Jewish incarnations
was united conceptually from without into yet a third denomination:
Orthodoxy. The great *yeshivas* (Talmudic academies), the Hasidic
communities, religious Zionists, Agudath Israel, the Young Israel—a
motley crew, indeed—were all heaped into the same pile. To be candid, they were identified much less in terms of what they were than of
what they were not.

The lack of clarity and cohesion in this category bothered liberal
thinkers and social analysts very little. At best, these were merely
vestiges. Surely traditional religious beliefs and practices, by whatever
designation, could not survive the pressures and strains of an open
society.

Groups noted primarily for their obscurantism, groups by their nature isolationist, parochial and backward-looking, would not take root
in the American soil. Most likely, Orthodoxy would soon die from
natural causes. At the least, it would meld itself into one of the other
two branches of Judaism in the United States or remain the identity of
those few pietists who always live at the edge of a modern society.

III

Somehow it just didn't happen that way. What was assumed to be
a death rattle was more a loud groan in response to the pangs of a

difficult adjustment. Accommodation is frequently less painful than transplantation. And, of course, every transplantation requires some accommodation. But the stricter the adherence to old ways, the less "give" there is, the longer and more difficult must be the process. Dormancy was too easily mistaken for expiration. Those very factors that were understood as reactionary and obscurantist were also stabilizing. There appears to have been more vitality than was earlier imputed in the authoritative consistency that Orthodoxy came to represent. In any event, its tenacity is impressive.

Certainly, part of the picture was framed by external events. The Holocaust and its ramifications, for example, had profound impact. Its attack on the very legitimacy of the Jew, its negation of the Jew's humanity, served as a shock. The shock was deeply felt, even by those who took their Jewishness for granted, indeed even by those who saw it as passé. The events were too raw to be ignored.

The plight of the survivors as displaced persons and their slow trickle into the United States made the tragedy still more graphic. The handful of East European sages who arrived, along with remnants of once flourishing Hasidic communities, offered a tangible motivation to sympathetically reconsider one's Jewish heritage. This small but significant immigration also helped reinforce already existing but not yet self-conscious Orthodox beachheads.

While these bastions of the religious right were regrouping, Orthodoxy's more liberal elements took strength from the birth of the State of Israel in the wake of the tragedy. To be sure, most Zionists were secular or agnostic in their personal beliefs and observances, but the very notion of Jewish nationalism and its rebirth on the ancestral homeland was at its base a deeply religious affair.

Zionism fulfilled messianic longings as much as political aspirations. It meant acting on Biblical prophecies and rabbinic dicta long eradicated from the world view of liberal Jewry, even as they had been formally repudiated by many U.S. Jewish leaders. Most of all, it was a negation of the millenial Diaspora, an unwillingness to negotiate with the temptations of an alien environment no matter how hospitable. The United States may have been the "goldene medinah," but it should never be mistaken for a permanent home.

In Israel, traditional Jewish practice would be written into the basic law of the infant polity and would frame the fabric of daily discourse. The impact of socialism upon Zionist thinking notwithstanding, Israel's religious establishment would eschew liberalism in favor of *halakah*, Jewish law applied to the needs of a modern state. In this sense, Zionism could do nothing but vitalize modern Orthodoxy even as its adherents referred to it in their prayers as "the first blossom of the Redemption."

But it would be one more generation before these early seeds bore fruit. U.S. Jewry's more liberal elements rose and mobilized in the immediate postwar years. By contrast, Orthodox communities, concentrated largely in the old ethnic neighborhoods of the Northeast, were just coming to terms with their new residences.

Stresses and strains marked the relationship between the arrival of Holocaust survivors and those Orthodox who were children of immigrants. The former had been painfully uprooted from their East European homes and longed bitterly for the intensely Jewish environments that had been destroyed before their very eyes. They had come to the United States unwillingly, with no dreams, no aspirations. Their adjustment would be slower and more difficult than normal.

By the same token, Orthodox institutions and religious bodies were still in their formative stages. They would undergo substantial change and innovation that would later make them surprisingly robust, though at times anomalous to the American model. But, as yet, they were unsuited to compete for broad communal leadership.

The individual move toward professionalism and higher education was not yet visible within Orthodoxy in the immediate postwar years. More secular and liberal Jewish elements had already distinguished themselves at the universities and in the professions, despite restrictive quotas and latent anti-Semitism, but such mobility would not be prominent within Orthodoxy for another generation.

Today, however, Jewish traditionalism in the United States—and its institutional manifestation as Orthodoxy—has returned with a passion. Witness for example, the growth of affluent, suburban, professional, Orthodox Jewish communities outside large urban centers throughout the country.

While most householders, male and female, commute into a city for their livelihood, each community is ritually self-sufficient. Many include a *mikvah* or ritualarium, and an *eruv*, a theological device that eases certain Sabbath restrictions and has particular appeal for parents of young children.

In addition, restaurants, butcher shops, and take-home catering es-

In addition, restaurants, butcher shops, and take-home catering establishments are common, each operating under recognized *glatt* (smooth) kosher supervision. Local religious schools of surprisingly high caliber have been established in most communities, and in the more progressive, a ritually correct tennis club or health spa can be found.

Witness, as well, the growing number of Orthodox interns, residents, house staff, and attending physicians at major metropolitan hospitals and medical centers throughout the country and, similarly, the broad presence of Orthodox men and women on university faculties, in law, and in accounting firms, indeed in all phases of their callings. Unlike many of their predecessors, these people are less concerned about attracting attention to themselves and their personal practices. Men are quite likely to don the *kippah*, the traditional skull cap, at the office, in the classroom, or at the clinic. For some it has become a mark of pride and self-respect. Others hardly even think about it.

The presence of this new cadre of young Orthodox professionals is outdone by their visibility. It is almost a monument to their lack of self-conscious discomfort. They have established structures to support their religious needs in some of the stodgiest, most hidebound of places. Kosher food is commonplace today at business meetings and university cafeterias. Many metropolitan financial districts have afternoon services at a given board room or conference chamber. An equal number of medical centers have afternoon classes and study sessions in Talmud or the weekly Bible readings, with commentaries.

IV

Consider, as well, the proliferation of thriving institutions and programs geared toward the Ba'al Teshuva, those penitents who return to Judaism in both practice and outlook. Whether emphasizing prayer, study, outreach, or support services, the spectrum extends from the Chabad Community to Yeshiva University, from Rabbi Shlomo Carlebach to Rabbi Shlomo Riskin.

The emergence of this new population of ritually observant Jews is worth a brief digression. Although they make up only a small percentage of Jewish youth, those who return have been highly visible in some of the most unlikely places. Even at isolated U.S. Jewish outposts there are stories of children who caught the spark while attending some youth program, study tour, or social gathering. Often the entire community takes vicarious pride in the achievement.

By some reciprocal calculus, many staid and traditional rabbinic seminaries have suddenly "discovered America." They have recognized that there is a large, unserviced constituency "out of town"— as they refer to any place more than one hour's drive from New York City. The potential for winning converts also represents new sources for student recruitment and fund raising.

In response, seed programs, leadership seminars, and summer residencies have been introduced in all parts of the country. Participants are drawn from the big urban centers and the smaller rural communities alike. The primary intention is to expose locals to the joys of traditional Judaism, but these programs are also designed to expose future rabbis and educators to the realities of American Judaism.

The impact of those who return has been felt as much in Israel as in the United States. Many of these young pietists have found religion on a mission to the Holy Land. Perhaps the visit was their first systematic confrontation with Jewish culture. Indeed, it was for that precise reason that their parents consented to the trip.

The result can be unintended, however. Though a distinct minority, some will commit themselves to months, even years of study in one of Jerusalem's Ba'al Teshuva academies. They will assume the dress and speech of Hasidic or yeshiva life, depend upon others to choose mates and occupations for them, and join a closed community. This is much to the dismay of well-meaning parents who sent them.

Though their numbers are substantially fewer than those who leave the fold, the very presence and visibility of the Ba'al Teshuva makes an important statement. It suggests that despite the rhetoric of the past, there is a clear place for traditional Judaism in the United States. It is a point well worth reflection.

The assumptions of a generation ago notwithstanding, assimilation into the mainstream appears not to have answered everyone's needs, despite the cultural and material riches this country has to offer. There are those who have been reared well within its bounds but who have been been drawn to the traditional faith of their fathers—or, more properly, the traditional faith abandoned by their fathers.

This thinking is reciprocal. At many holiday gatherings sponsored by Ba'al Teshuva institutions both here and in Israel, interested outsiders are invited to participate. Ironically, such events draw large numbers of Orthodox onlookers, people who are not themselves among the newly penitent, yet who are fascinated all the same.

Certainly, there is an attraction, almost a bit of spectacle, in any public display of the odd and unusual. There is a sensationalism in observing these "born-again" Jews performing well-worn rituals with freshness and emotional commitment. Too often, such devotion is absent in the observers' own practice. It has become far too routine. But these observers also gain support for their own feelings by watching the Ba'al Teshuva affirming their beliefs. Despite their Orthodoxy, even the most isolated stand subject to confrontations with the general culture. Moreover, their lifestyles were set out for them from earliest childhood. They take great satisfaction in watching those who have come to these beliefs as adults, those who have been drawn to them voluntarily.

Consider what may be the most telling change in the status of Orthodoxy. In radical contrast to the circumstances of a decade or so ago, there are now growing numbers of Orthodox professionals in the Jewish communal service. Many hold positions of authority within well-established Jewish volunteer organizations of clearly non-Orthodox history, membership, and inclination.

The point was driven home rather sardonically by a leader of one such organization recently. Just prior to the opening of a meeting of the Conference of Presidents of Major Jewish Organizations, this veteran of "the Jewish wars" surveyed the attendance and the affiliations of those taking their seats around the long conference table. "Only in America," he said, shaking his head in disbelief, "only in America."

In a sense, the renewal of Orthodoxy in a young, growing, and surprisingly vibrant segment of the U.S. Jewish community may be understood pragmatically. Whatever the perceived needs of two generations ago, things have changed. Perhaps liberal and progressive theology and decisions to formally discard practice and ritual are no longer waves of the future for a qualitatively significant portion of U.S. Jews.

Compromise and accommodation were initiated in the hope of attracting the youth and making the better educated, the acculturated, more comfortable in a familiar religious setting, but it appears that neither the young nor the upwardly mobile stormed the gates of the synagogues as a result, nor did they flood the study halls and seminaries.

One need not belabor the growing rates of secularism, assimilation,

and intermarriage, and documentation is not required for the threat
posed by cults of all variety. For our purposes, however, it must be
emphasized that these problems are far more pronounced among Jews
whose ties to tradition, Judaic spirit, and culture are tenuous and con-
fused.

The exodus from tradition, therefore, is fast losing much of the
utilitarian imperative that it once claimed. Those whose response is to
further deviate from tradition in the hope of reclaiming their younger
and more progressive elements are probably in for a shock. If anything, the contemporary mood dictates the reverse.

Nevertheless, these initial accommodations have now been institutionalized, probably past their utility. If by nothing other than the measure of pragmatism, they may be compared to the European-imported
Orthodoxy of two generations ago. Both appeared unsuited to their
environments but each claimed the allegiance of devotees who clung
out of sincere, if misguided principle.

Of course, what has developed as U.S. Orthodoxy of the 1980s is
also the result of compromise, dervied from the same professional values and social aspirations that motivated liberals a generation earlier.
Personal religious practices aside, one cannot attend a university or
professional school without being affected. One cannot participate in
the secular arena and not be influenced. One cannot taste the material
benefits of affluence and not undergo change.

In addition, what has emerged as an Orthodox renewal today is
partly a reflection of increased interest in traditional religion generally,
both within the United States and throughout the world. For example,
the recent explosion of religious fundamentalism, particularly, though
not exclusively, throughout the Muslim world, is well known. Its link
to Arab radicalism and terror has made it the major political dynamic
of the past decade.

By the same token, evangelists have emerged as national figures in
the United States appearing in media far removed from their traditional
Bible Belt constituencies. Prayer meetings are held on campuses
throughout the country, as well as on the steps of the White House.
Religious figures are consulted on political issues, and public officials
make reference to the demands of God and Scripture in formulating
public policy. It should come as no surprise, therefore, that a segment
of U.S. Jewry is influenced similarly.

Whatever its source, today's Orthodoxy is far removed from that of the elders. Its mission is to confront the challenges of modern material values and popular culture, both directly and indirectly. While not defeating them, it appears to be demonstrating that they are not incompatible, per se, with Jewish observance and ritual.

The proliferation of continental and Oriental eateries, Carribean cruises, and exotic Passover vacation packages—all under strict rabbinic supervision—serves witness to the fact that an upscale consumer need not compromise ritual demands. The presence of prayer services and Talmud classes at metropolitan hospitals, university campuses, and financial districts makes the same point. One need not live in seclusion nor deny the world.

V

Nevertheless, these developments are new, strange, and still fluid. All is not perfectly well with them. In some cases they result in an insecurity and confusion. One senses a longing, an internal conflict as newfound indulgences require that some liberties be taken with the spirit, if not the letter, of the law.

Among the more astute, there is a gnawing doubt about the authenticity of it all. Even among the less astute, there is an equally conspicuous attempt to regain some of the simple piety of an earlier age. Be it spiritual, be it nostalgic, perhaps even vicarious, it is real. In the words of one veteran Jewish educator: "There is no reason why the young Jewish child of America cannot equal his European predecessor in all aspects of Torah study." Perhaps so, but why would he want to, aside from this longing to idealize the past?

In what may be an overreaction, many of the best-educated and most affluent among today's assertive Orthodox have adopted surprisingly rightward orientations toward their own ritual observance and that of their family. They have opted for strictly devout curricula and highly segregated social settings in the education of their children, and they have sought clergy and religious functionaries with the most classical religious training.

That parents seek to provide a superior upbringing for their children is surely well within the best familial traditions of the past. In many ways it is part of the cultural baggage that early immigrants brought with them to these shores, but these aspirations have generally been defined in material terms.

Here the bent is different. Perhaps they are disturbed by lacunae in their own training; perhaps they have been disaffected by the heavy-handed methods they encountered. As they look back on their own Jewish education, they are left cold and uninspired.

The issues they would confront on campus and in the "real world" were dealt with peripherally, if at all. They entered universities and professional schools with a childish view of their religious beliefs. It was one that could easily be exploded by not so well meaning faculty and colleagues.

The commitment to Jews elsewhere was rarely explored. The social and theological implications of the birth of the State of Israel were virtually ignored. An inordinate amount of time was spent with the rudiments of ritual observance, at the expense of ethical and moral values. The events of history, especially contemporary history, and the role of the Jew within them were a matter of ad hoc treatment and general indifference.

At the same time, they exhibit a disenchantment with their experiences in this real world of higher education and professional achievement. They are less impressed with modernity and sophistication, perhaps for not having to fight the ideological battles of the past. The very cosmopolitan progressivism that is usually associated with upward mobility and affluence has become passé.

These parents seek a better, more comprehensively Jewish environment for their children. They seek a modern and enlightened educational methodology along with a strictly traditional curriculum. If they cannot better prepare their children, then they would like to shield them altogether from these tensions and disappointments.

In some instances the tension results in an active involvement with local Jewish schools. The goal is to help introduce programs that are sophisticated and socially aware and to engage instructors able to implement them. Even at the primary level, there have been innovations in Holocaust studies, Zionism, Jewish life abroad, Jewish philosophy, and Jewish history. Some have taken students out of the classroom to rallies and protests, to local communal institutions, and to programs of study abroad, notably in Israel.

In other instances, parents have been moved to send their children to schools far to the religious right of their own training and lifestyle. Their hope is to provide, thereby, a stronger and more secure Jewish foundation for their families and a less vulnerable weltanschauung than they have themselves. The more insulated the early training, the more comprehensive and complete will be the Jewish commitment.

In truth, the results are often ironic and almost humorous. Picture the well-dressed and cosmopolitan suburban parent walking to synagogue on a given Sabbath. At each hand is a teenage son whose attire—black suit, tieless white shirt, and broad-brimmed black hat— makes the family portrait incongruous, to say the least.

Or consider professionals whose children opt out entirely. For them, any form of secular pursuit is a wasteful indulgence, even sinful. Rather than "make something" of themselves, as their parents had always hoped they would, they spend their years in a yeshiva community, immersed in full-time study of ancient Jewish texts. The Lord will provide.

Similarly, affluent and upwardly mobile parents are having daughters who choose to marry such a young man and live within the confines of the kolel. Here, the husband continues his postgraduate Jewish education, living with his growing family on the grounds of the academy. The couple depends upon small stipends, the efforts of the wife, and parental largesse to underwrite their material needs. Mama and Papa will provide.

There are those who take these developments kindly. They are, after all, a part of the very renewal of which we speak. Others wonder if the time, effort, and funds expended in these directions are efficiently utilized. Both observations are probably correct. In a more direct sense, however, parents who regret this turn in their children must recognize that the early education chosen for their offspring goes a long way in determining what kind of adults they become. Once past adolescence, it—and the peer group it provides—is probably the singular influence in a child's life. Parents must realize that whatever tensions have arisen are of their own making.

VI

Despite its growth, far beyond the expectations of most observers a generation ago, Orthodoxy is by no means taking over. In many ways, outward visibility is deceptive. Most studies suggest that it accounts for no more than about 10 percent of the U.S. Jewish population. The data is based on self-identification, that is, those who subjectively des-

ignate themselves as Orthodox. Individual levels of observance or belief are doubtless much lower.

It must be noted that Orthodoxy's relative success in recent years
has not been without social cost. In particular, contemporary Orthodox
communities have exhibited three disturbing characteristics: (1) an in-
sular tendency toward the rest of the Jewish community, (2) a penchant for stratification along lines of religious observance within Orthodoxy itself, and (3) the wild growth of institutional power and
affiliation to undergird the other two.

There are many factors contributing to these tendencies. They may
be a "so there!" reaction to the eulogies that were erroneously delivered to Orthodoxy in the past. They may be part of the growing pains
that accompany any process of maturation. Perhaps they are related to
variables in the general culture, within which they are but guests. No
matter the source, they are disturbing all the same.

The manifestations are commonplace. One is the inability, or rather
unwillingness, to work together with Jews who do not share their religious values. Orthodox Jews too often avoid broad councils of domestic and international Jewish welfare, if participation will require
that they share the podium with spokespeople of deviating theological
doctrine. There is a profound unwillingness to proffer any implicit
legitimacy, be its social, organizational, or ideological, to these competing branches of Judaism, even when the issues are neutral or all-
embracing. It is only very recently, and very haltingly, that some have
deigned to involve themselves in programs of Zionist or philanthropic
concern. Even here, participation has generally been individual, and
those who have participated have often been subject to abuse and os-
tracism themselves.

Aside from the importance of unity in confronting overarching concerns, the lack is also counterproductive from a self-interested perspective. Most issues that face U.S. Jews do not easily divide themselves by the degree of one's religious observance or doctrinal purity.
Further, those outside Judaism do not and will not understand that
which separates the Jewish community. The already free proliferation
of public dissent within Judaism needs no further impetus.

By the same token, powerful and well-established Jewish organizations make important fiscal and monetary policy regarding issues of
vital importance to the Orthodox Jewish community. These include aid
to religious schools, child care, elder care, housing subsidy, and the
like. Such organizations will not be moved easily from without.

They certainly will not be moved by external indifference or condescending arrogance. Concerns about lending passive legitimacy are real. So is the fear of co-optation. However, Jewish survival will not be realized in a vacuum. Much can be derived from joint effort without necessarily impinging upon ideological loyalties, loyalties that may actually be irrelevant to the issues at hand.

The tendency has an internal equivalent. Much of Orthodoxy has seen fit to strategically insulate itself in order to support its integrity vis-à-vis a material and secular society, but a highly structured system of stratification has also emerged within Orthodoxy itself. Status here cuts in several overlapping directions. Some are superficial, for example, dress, speech, or fashion. Others reach backward toward geneology and the region from which the family stemmed. Still others relate to the stringency of religious observance, alongside salient choices of residence and education. In any event, members of the Orthodox community have segmented themselves in a variety of ways.

To be sure, many of these divisions existed before. Differences between German and East European Jews have already been discussed. So too have there always been cleavages among Jews of Hasidic descent and between students of one or another academy of Jewish learning.

For the most part, sentiments were transported from Eastern Europe and then bent to fit the new environment. And for the most part, they lost much of their bite as the passing generations made them irrelevant. In a few exceptions, notably within the Hasidic communities, what once were mild dislikes have been transformed into battles of doctrine and faith.

It must also be recalled that the standard unit of analysis is crude. The designation of everyone to the religious right of the Conservative movement as "Orthodox" enforces a high degree of diversity and incongruity within that category. The problem may be less in the subject than in the analyst.

Yet aside from, and more disturbing than, these horizontal divisions is a vertical caste that revolves about many of the same issues of ritual observance and family history. The structure has become so evident that even casual observers of Orthodoxy commonly refer to its "right-wing," "centrist," and "modern" branches, among others.

Once again, tendencies in elementary parochial education offer an interesting example. Individual schools pride themselves on the exclusivity of their student body. Children from the "wrong" kinds of families are discouraged, and parents can feel assured that their children will move in the desired social circles.

Parents will severely criticize their school—to the point of transferring their children—should its administration attempt to be more pluralistic. But, the "wrong" elements of Orthodoxy are frequently people of marginal socioeconomic or ethnic status (for example, new immigrants) who may need most what the school has to offer. Individual institutions must cater to their needs exclusively, thus segregating them still further.

Similarly, it is not unknown for a school administration to publish a list of religious requisites imposed upon parents who choose to send their children to its classes. Homes are inspected, and parents are required to adopt certain modes of dress and to make important social choices in conforming to school policy. Sanctions are social but very effective, nonetheless.

That individuals have the right to voluntarily regiment themselves in this way is not at issue. The concern is their condescension and self-righteousness toward those who have chosen otherwise. What results is an active and often hostile stratification that weakens an already small community and saps a good bit of its potential.

Perhaps the most unfortunate example of this phenomenon is the attitude toward the newcomers to Orthodoxy, the Ba'al Teshuva. As noted above, these penitents, though a tiny proportion of America's Jews, are important for their visibility and for the symbolic statement they make. One would expect that they be show-cased and afforded high honor for their importance to the community. Often they are, but just as often, they suffer a painful stigma when facing important choices. If single, then they may not be seen as appropriate mates for those who come from the mainstream. Indeed, organizations and agencies geared toward their outreach frequently attempt to match them with others of similar experience. It may make good social sense, but it reinforces the segregation and polite condescension of which we speak.

A similar fate attaches to those who return to Orthodoxy as a family, that is, in midlife and with children. It is surely heartwarming for Orthodox leaders to see the family join its ranks as a unit. The change is often the result of a youth program through which the children later draw their elders. However, in seeking a mate, these same children may suffer for their efforts. They, too, are often unsuitable for the more traditional elements of the community. Their ritual and theological choices may be laudatory, but alas, they have no *yichus*, no proper lineage.

As might be expected, the tendency has imprinted itself upon the internal values and self-image of many within Orthodoxy. It takes the form of a fixation with what lurks over the right shoulder. To be sure, an innate sense of free-floating guilt has been popularly associated with U.S. Jewish life for decades, but here it looks like something akin to communal paranoia.

While crude systems of classification insure great diversity and important divisions within the fold, Orthodoxy is nothing if not a community of values. There may be many lapses in practice, but most are the result of convenience rather than principle. In this sense, there is great truth in a recent insight offered by the humorist, George Carlin. An Irish Catholic by birth, Carlin claims that he did not leave the church for reasons of deep moral or theological principle. Rather, he proclaims, "I just hate getting up early on Sundays!"

Yet, while deviations exist in practice, there is broad consensus on the rudiments of doctrine. Therein lies a key. The more important is the Orthodox affiliation, the more salient will be the social sanctions at its command and the more stinging will be the criticism, overt or implied, of those to one's religious right—even if the object of the critique is more a matter of custom and style than central precept.

This, of course, need not suggest a shift in behavior or even attitude. In fact, hostility and rejection may be the most common response to arrogance and self-righteousness, but the hostility, no matter how genuine, is mixed with nagging doubt and gnawing guilt. Guilt rarely commands behavior; it merely prevents one from enjoying his deviations.

Especially for those close to large Orthodox centers, concern for appearance and outward practice has become a commonplace. Even those of moderate bent are asking, "What will the right wing say?" In some settings, neighbors outdo each other with their respective ritual stringencies. Their sages are pressed to seek still higher forms of purity to match the spiraling demands of congregants.

These conspicuous displays of external piety are often matched by similar shows of material success. Fine silver and gold adorn objects of personal Judaica and ritual use even as they adorn the wrists and necklines of the users. Parochial school tuitions rise each year as do the prices of the designer clothes that their students wear. The competition for religious and social status is both frenzied and expensive, calling upon the adherent to find ever more creative ways to pay for it all.

Most shocking in this regard, is the ease by which ritual devotion is separated from personal ethic, where business success underwrites piety. In the recent past, the Orthodox community has been wracked by a litany of high corruption including mistreatment of the resident elderly at proprietary institutions of long-term care, laundering of illegal funds through the financial offices of religious institutions and academies of higher learning, stock fraud, commercial forgery, smuggling and more. One must be concerned for a belief-system whose adherents readily compartmentalize between religious practice and simple honesty or worse yet, where the latter serves the ends of the former.

It's easy to be swept away in it all. Liberal values—be they social, religious, or political—are increasingly hard to come by, and the flexibility to respond to new issues as they arise is drowned in a deluge of guilt and fear, something akin to communal paranoia.

Finally, the race toward exemplary religious practice has spawned a variety of organizational affiliations. With each institution representing another shading of practice or belief, the essential mission is to cement these newfound social and ideological tendencies. With it comes the capacity to destroy much of the vitality that lent Orthodoxy its resurgence from the first. Each has its own presidium and distinguished trustees; each has its religious and ideological leadership; each claims to preserve the heritage of another slice of this rather limited pie. It simply isn't enough to be Orthodox, to conform to a religious ideology or ritual. Values and practice must also be organized by card-carrying, dues-paying membership.

In an important sense, this is characteristic of U.S. Jewish life in general. The proliferation of organizations, committees, and fraternal units is legion. Umbrella agencies unite member organizations, and commissions provide forums for leaders of umbrella agencies. And so it goes.

Indeed, the penchant for institutionalization has invaded the house of worship itself. Many large Orthodox synagogues, unconsciously perhaps, have followed their Reform and Conservative counterparts in regard to architecture and design. They measure their importance by the size of their chapels or the capacity of their catering facilities.

The style of worship has followed suit. There is greater concern for propriety and silence. Permanent places are assigned, and those who seek more extemporaneous expression are told to sit down. Children are said to disturb the service, while the women are said to be too noisy. Heavy-handed strategists control them both as decorum committees are formed to set and enforce ever more stringent policy.

In response, many young families have sought membership in small congregations known as *shteeblach*, literally, small rooms. Largely confined to urban centers, a *shteeb'l* may be privately owned or cooperatively organized. But whatever its organizational design, there are several distinctive aspects to its worship.

Here the service is less formal, the dues more manageable, and the environment less threatening. Policy is more democratic and participation quite open. By the same token, the service is noisy, the level of concentration none too impressive, and the children unruly. But the emergence of these homey congregations is indirect reaction to the overbearing qualities common in more formal houses of worship.

The reaction of larger, mainstream synagogues has been predictable. They could evaluate their own practices and introduce some that are friendlier and more hospitable. They could inquire into the success of these shteeblach and consider some of the qualities that make them attractive. Instead they label them a threat, and perhaps they are.

This trend toward institutionalization may be the most destructive of all. At the communal level it reinforces social stratification, serves a segmented constituency, and competes for limited public resources. It legitimates an already evident tendency toward insularity by providing parallel institutions and creating an independent (redundant) dynamic of its own.

At the local level it serves to constrain those elements of Orthodoxy that have provided it with newfound momentum. Noise and tumult, even in the midst of prayer and religious devotion, are signs of growth and vitality. Many who have had the experience will affirm that there is nothing particularly attractive about a silent synagogue.

Orthodoxy's recent successes are the result of its fluidity and youthful vibrance. These are characteristics that must be guarded, nurtured, and encouraged. If the success is to be sustained, if it is to flourish, then they ought not to be sacrificed on the altars of social insularity, religious stratification, and organizational design.

4

Republicans, Democrats, and U.S. Jews

I

One of the immutable laws of U.S. politics is the Jewish link to liberalism and the Democratic party. Jewish voters are consistently more likely to choose liberal candidates, to hold liberal positions, and to support liberal causes than are their gentile cohorts in the U.S. population. To the extent that the Democratic party is equated in Jewish minds with this liberalism, it has been the beneficiary of their political preferences since the beginning of the century.

Study after study has suggested the tenacity of this preference, even when such actions appear contrary to Jewish social and economic self-interest. This preference has ignored generational and regional differences to become a virtual given of U.S. electoral politics, whether national or local.

Several theories have been posited to explain the phenomenon. Some suggest that Jewish political liberalism is the direct offshoot of traditional Jewish values. Concern for the poor, a generally optimistic view of man's place in the world, and support for educational and cultural pursuits are said to be basics of Jewish religious thinking. Transferring them to the fertile soil of these United States naturally resulted in their application to the secular political context. What emerged was a Jewish link to liberal thinking.

Others demur. That being the case, they note dryly, those most familar with or most committed to Jewish values should express greater liberalism than those distant from the tradition. In fact, the opposite appears to be true. The more ritually observant members of the Jewish community, those steeped in its rites and learned in its classical lore, tend to be the most conservative, both socially and intellectually. The roots of Jewish liberalism are historical rather than theological, they argue. On the one hand, they reflect the timing and the substance of Jewish migration to the United States. They also bear the mark of the Jewish confrontation with modern European political and intellectual culture. The combination of these elements over the past century or so helped socialize the Jewish community to the outside world.

For the most part, Jews were allowed to participate in West European national politics, outside the confines of their corporate communities, only with the dawn of the Napoleonic era. In Eastern Europe, their participation would occur with violent eruptions decades later. In either case, the alternatives available to them were extraordinarily narrow.

Nobility, royalists, conservatives, and the like could never ignore millenia of hatred and bigotry. They liked Jews no more than before, no matter what the prevailing political currents dictated. Certainly, they had great difficulty welcoming Jews into their social and political circles or appealing to their interests in any formal coalition.

Rather, those Jews who would participate were shunted toward the more radical elements of the political spectrum, those whose very raison d'être was a rejection of the old order and a call for its destruction. It was no accident, therefore, that Jews, newly and haltingly liberated from the ghettos and *shtetlach* of Europe, were disproportionately found among socialist, anarchist, and radical thinkers in Europe during the nineteenth and early twentieth centuries.

When they arrived in the United States, many brought their Marxism and socialism with them. This is not to suggest that they came as revolutionaries. Quite the contrary, most simply wanted to improve their lot. But they brought important symbols of their new political interests. They quickly became an active presence in the U.S. labor movement, for example, notably within the needle trades and light industries of the Northeast.

For many years, the Yiddish *Daily Forward*, flagship publication of the immigrant Jewish community, prominently carried the socialist slogan "Workers of the World Unite, You Have Nothing to Lose but Your Chains!" The Yiddish radio station in New York adopted WEVD as its call letters, initials of the legendary U.S. socialist leader, Eugene V. Debs.

Many of the same factors that socialized Jewish entry into politics in Europe were also at play on these shores. Republicans, the party of business, privilege, and political reform, had little use for the riffraff that was being attracted to this land of opportunity. Captains of industry might recruit unskilled workers from their midst, but they hesitated to seek voters and political colleagues among them.

By contrast, urban Democrats were led by the children of Irish immigrants. If only for their own political needs, they found it easier to welcome this new class of supporters and to help them through some of the rougher spots on their road toward integration. In so doing, they also convinced their new wards to register and vote—often, if possible.

Jewish immigrants, or at least many of those with political consciousness upon arrival, were already predisposed toward liberalism, even radicalism. Their nurture, under the auspices of an urban Democratic machine, furthered the tendency. The grand coalition of their children, as academics, intellectuals, or union activists, behind the leadership of Franklin Roosevelt put a seal to it all. When FDR died, many Jews wore black. For them a great friend had passed on.

As a result of these and analogous experiences, the link between Jews and liberalism was well grounded. Its political and electoral expression through the Democratic party became an established fact. Soon it was transformed into a self-fulfilling prophecy. Over the years, Democratic presidential candidates carried 70 percent and more of the Jewish vote. In local elections, the majorities reached 90 percent. Little political savvy was required to predict the attitudes and the direction of financial support that moved with it.

In return, the Democratic party was alert to Jewish issues. In the domestic arena, there were support for organized labor and concern for individual and civil rights. Internationally, there followed a commitment to fight fascist anti-Semitism in Europe and, later, to support the military and economic security of the State of Israel. Democrats have always been in the forefront of issues close to the heart of the Jewish electorate. This, too, was easily predictable.

II

In more recent times, however, the relationship between Jewish voters and thinkers, on the one hand, and liberal ideals and the Democratic party, on the other, has changed profoundly. Sociologically and demographically, much of the past has simply passed and many of the historical circumstances that contributed to their linkage exist no more. On political grounds, that is, by dint of basic self-interest, their goals and objectives have diverged. What may once have been a grand coalition has become an anachronism, a cultural lag.

Aside from the historical forces at work, for a generation of immigrants and their children, liberal causes also suited rational political needs. A community seeking to integrate itself into a new society needs help in opening stubborn doors held shut by bigotry and discrimination. Organizing and lobbying to that end was raised to a sacred mission.

There were many doors closed to Jews in this country, whether at resorts or medical schools, banks or residential neighborhoods. Prying them open was a battle that justified the use of all legal means and political coalitions at hand. The Jewish leadership was quick to recognize that its argument would be that much more compelling if it included, under its umbrella, the needs of other minorities and immigrant groups in search of legal and social remedy. The lesson carried beyond immediate Jewish interests and soon became a matter of principle as much as pragmatism.

So, too, support for trade unions. As noted above, the Jewish identification with organized labor in the United States developed early upon their simultaneous arrivals. For a community that was made up largely of workers and toilers, such activism made good sense. It allowed them to join forces with others of similar needs under the union banner and helped them target political candidates with analogous sympathies and ethnosocial background.

But much of this is no more. The data have already been presented elsewhere. Suffice it to say that economically and professionally, U.S. Jews stand well in the lead among ethnic communities in this country. They are well-educated, affluent, and upwardly mobile. They have left their proletarian roots well behind and outpaced even the gentile majority that tried so hard to exclude them. Among their younger contingents, a staggering 80 percent hold professional or managerial positions.

Most of the civil rights battles no longer affect U.S. Jews. Newer initiatives, such as affirmative action or equal employment opportunity programs, have a negative effect, given their disproportionate presence in academia and in the professions. Attempts to integrate their schools and their communities have resulted in social confrontation and real soul-searching.

In many ways, what has changed is not so much Jewish attitudes but the context of liberalism. It is a shift set into motion in the 1960s and linked early on with campus rebellion and the antiwar movement. But within, it holds a restiveness that has not yet run its course.

Faced with increasing black activism, many liberals found themselves confronting militance beyond their control. Jewish interests, in particular, were often identified, directly or by implication, with the evil to be eradicated. Their desire to work within the system was attacked as establishment liberalism and as the thinking of the "old Left." The Jewish position, but a few steps removed from its humble beginnings, was at odds with those just beneath.

Jewish liberals found themselves as landlords and small retailers, social workers and teachers, in communities seeking to rid themselves of all such symbols of external repression. Expressions of civil rage and violence have historically meant trouble for Jews, no matter what their source. Here the confrontation was direct, and it chilled the spine of even the most committed Jewish liberal.

Though it had its genesis in the turbulence of the late 1960s, these shockwaves are still felt in the mid-1980s. Nowhere has it been more evident than in the single issue that stands as the hallmark of contemporary U.S. liberalism: civil rights and the status of black America.

Consider, for example, the 1984 presidential elections and the candidacy of Rev. Jesse Jackson. Tension between Jackson and Jewish leaders was evident from the first. Ethnic slurs attributed to him set the tone for the Democratic convention. His well-publicized suggestions that the United States should rethink its Middle East policy in favor of the needs of the Arab world and the rumor that contributions had been received from oil sheikhdoms interested in such a change infuriated Jewish leaders.

The thought that these might not be solitary incidents but only the tip of the iceberg visible to the media was soon grossly inflated. After all, the chosen Democratic candidate, former Vice-President Walter Mondale, had little chance of winning the general election. Jackson and his gaffes became the most exciting thing the party had to offer. For many, the problem was not Jackson's opinions of Jews. Nor was there much surprise in his criticism of Israel, though it was unprecedented among Democrats vying for their party's nod. He had never been circumspect about his feelings, and it was clear to whom his appeals were directed. What was most disturbing was the impotence of other major candidates, who were unwilling to distance themselves from Jackson and his rainbow coalition for fear of alienating minority voters. The party that had so long attracted the support of Jewish voters was now a captive of other interests, and the welfare of its Jewish constituency seemed of little consequence.

This phenomenon is neither short-term nor isolated; Jackson's presence will undoubtedly be felt in future elections. It is all part of the tension within contemporary liberalism, and the tenacity of this political confrontation has major implications for the U.S. Jewish community. But it is only part of the story.

His words notwithstanding, Jackson's political style is genteel and polished, but there was nothing genteel about the words of his staunch loyalist, Minister Louis Farrakhan, leader of the Nation of Islam. The profound changes in the context of liberalism became brutally clear to most U.S. Jews through his much publicized persona. Over the period of the election and its aftermath, Farrakhan attracted audiences and honoraria well into the thousands. He appeared at large university campuses and metropolitan convention centers in such major cities as Detroit, Atlanta, Washington, D.C., Los Angeles, and New York. At all of his lectures, he inspired his listeners with a message of economic renewal and self-help for the black community.

But his remarks were also peppered with comments about Jews as oppressors, as the founders of the slave trade, and as a greedy and corrupt people whose economic manipulations were all that prevented blacks from helping themselves. To be sure, his rhetoric inflamed already sensitive relations between the two groups. It was still more infuriating to watch black leaders, many of whom owed their positions and their successes at least in part to Jewish support, walk gingerly around the issue. As with the Democratic candidates noted above, they were hesitant to distance themselves from Farrakhan's political and social influence. They feared that in so doing they might alienate themselves from their own people and appear as though they were yielding to Jewish pressure.

Finally, there was yet another shift in liberalism with consequences for its Jewish patrons, and it emerged in the one political issue that most unites them: the safety and security of the State of Israel. Perhaps it has more to do with public relations. In part the shift results from a resurgence of political conservatism in Israel over the past decade, a factor that has eclipsed its liberal and socialist foundations. Perhaps it is little more than an instinctive liberal sympathy for the underdog, or for the side that has best succeeded in portraying itself as such.

For whatever reasons, Israel no longer appears to capture the imagination of liberal thinkers and intellectuals. By contrast, they appear more fired by the plight of the poor, homeless Palestinian, seeking only human rights and self-determination. A once passionate alliance is quickly passing by the wayside.

It is still possible for Jewish organizations to trot out an aging black leader or a member of the labor establishment, some of whose liberal credentials have themselves been subject to question. But formerly proud linkages between the liberal and civil rights communities and the Zionist corps in the United States have been subject to severe strain. This is true even when the representatives of the former are themselves Jewish.

Yet for the near future, the Jewish link to the Democratic party, at least at the national level, appears to be intact. A quick glance at the results of the 1984 election is illuminating. Despite all that has been said about Jackson and Farrakhan, despite the refusal of many Democratic and black leaders to repudiate them, and despite doubts about the integrity of their support for Israel, the results were predictable. The Democratic candidate was able to garner roughly two-thirds of the Jewish vote.

III

In contrast, a large portion of the U.S. electorate appears to have moved to the political right behind the popular leadership of Ronald Reagan, one of the first genuinely conservative presidents of the modern era. Jewish voters might be susceptible to a political change as well, Republican leaders have reasoned. They too are moved by the same national currents that brought about the Reagan landslides, and they have had to confront powerful changes within their own community of political interests. Perhaps their anchor to liberalism can be shaken.

To drive home the point, Republicans have moved to attract Jewish support both symbolically and substantively in the best way they know how. They have pledged loyalty to the welfare of the State of Israel as the single true democracy in the Middle East and as a bulwark against Communist expansion. It is a position that fits into President Reagan's view of a world neatly divided into two camps, and it is a view that has been encouraged by Israel's own resurgent right. While in some ways the attempt has the force of history behind it, one doubts that it will yield much of a return at the polls.

The position was transformed well beyond electoral rhetoric early in the Reagan administration. Israel's invasion of southern Lebanon, the subsequent dispatch of U.S. Marines as part of a supervisory force, and the Israeli occupation that lasted over two years opened a new era in U.S. support for the security of Israel and its military objectives. It has not been lost on U.S. Jews.

For many reasons, the war in Lebanon was protracted and painful. It was Israel's longest war, the first fought entirely on foreign soil, and one that gained it international notoriety. Israel suffered some six hundred casualties and several thousand wounded as a result less of the initial days of battle than the long months of occupation that followed. Its army camped in unfamiliar terrain facing guerrilla and terrorist forces supported by the local civilian population, albeit under duress. It was a war that drained the economy, costing some $1 million a day by the end of the occupation.

But perhaps most damaging of all, it was a war that raised moral doubts within Israel itself—doubts in regard to its objectives, in regard to the motives and machinations of its leadership, and in regard to atrocities perpetrated in territory under Israeli control. A commission of investigation was impaneled in its aftermath. Military and political leaders at the highest level were censured. Ultimately it led to the resignation of cabinet officials and contributed to the prime minister's retirement from active political life.

But if it was Israel's longest war, in part it was because U.S. leadership allowed it to be. Israeli military strategists have always depended upon lightning victories. In part, this was because of the overwhelming odds they faced and the limitations of their human and military resources. But it also stemmed from the sense that their playing time was severely limited and restricted by international pressure. Yet this time Israel's leadership was left unfettered by U.S. demands to pull back and mop up. For what may have been the first time in its history, the Israel Defense Force was given its head. New objectives were defined almost "on the fly," that is, after the initial victories of the first few days as no calls came from the United States to cease and desist.

To be sure, U.S. intentions were not only altruistic on Israel's behalf, nor were they primarily directed toward appeals to the U.S. Jewish voter, though they were used as such during and after the affair. Rather, there were powerful diplomatic and international motivations at work, motivations that reflected realpolitik as much as anything else.

Allowing Israel to beat up on Palestinian forces in Lebanon made good sense to the U.S. diplomatic and military corps on several grounds. First, it could be used as evidence for the superiority of U.S. military hardware as compared with that which the Soviets provided. Israel was employing U.S. matériel almost exclusively, while the other side had been armed by the Soviet Union directly or through its clients in Syria and Libya.

The defeat of Palestinian ground forces and the demolition of the Syrian air corps suggested to all who sought military aid anywhere in the world that it made good sense to deal with the United States and to respect those who were its allies. The reality, of course, was somewhat different, that is, it was U.S. armament in the hands of the Israelis that defeated Soviet hardware being utilized by various Arab forces. Still, the results were used to make the argument.

Related to this was the calculated assumption that neither the Soviet Union nor the bulk of the Arab world would rush to the support of their allies and cohorts in the Palestine Liberation Organization (PLO). Aside from blustery rhetoric from afar, Yassir Arafat's forces were left on their own, fighting the Israelis as well as the various militia that held small pockets of the Lebanese political vacuum. Even Syrian support was neither altruistic nor an unmixed blessing, as it later encouraged its Palestinian puppet to turn on the PLO central command.

Once again the events played into the hands of U.S. foreign policy. Without firing a shot, the diplomatic status of the United States rose throughout the Middle East as the Soviet Union and radical Arab re-

gimes looked on. As a result, the Soviet Union was effectively eliminated as a credible actor in the Middle East, relegated to supplying the
most radical and least stable of clients in the region. Whether in peace
or in war, it appeared that an alliance with the United States was the
only game in town.

Subsequent events in the Middle East have pushed the United States
and Israel still closer together. Largely because it has been identified
as the prime mover and supplier in Israeli military superiority, the
United States has become a target for Arab terror throughout the world.

U.S. citizens and military personnel, for example, have been subject to sniper fire, bombings, and hijackings in the civilized capitals
of Europe as well as within their air space or off their shores. Some
twenty-one U.S. diplomats have been murdered by Middle Eastern
terror since the advent of the Reagan administration, while others have
been kidnapped and held hostage, along with British, French, and Ital-
ian colleagues.

In contrast to the confusion and indecision of the Jimmy Carter years,
President Reagan won plaudits for establishing a tough posture toward
terrorists and those states that supply or shield them. A U.S. bombing
mission in Libya and a call for antiterrorist coordination among the
Western allies were the immediate results. Public investigation of links
between Middle Eastern terror and support for revolutionary movements in the Carribean, notably through Cuba and the Sandinista government in Nicaragua, were also initiated.

Alas, revelations of U.S. negotiations with Iran for the release of
hostages in southern Lebanon, however, have compromised a policy
that declared it would never capitulate to terror. The waning years of
the Reagan presidency will undoubtedly suffer from the resulting loss
of credibility linked to the natural weakness of a lame-duck administration. This is an issue that the president will not easily shake.

IV

Historical trends are not broken by events of the moment, however
powerful and profound though they may be. Jewish political predilic-
tions toward liberalism will survive, no matter how vigorously Republican leaders advertise their support for Israel or other issues dear to
the hearts of U.S. Jewish voters. Even short-term voting shifts will be

corrected as liberal tendencies reflect themselves over time or move from local to statewide and national races.

Additionally, there is a serious concern raised over the president's foreign policy, especially as it is reflected in many pockets of electoral support he received over the past few years. This has mitigated some of its positive effect on Jewish opinion. The chance that Jewish voters will switch to the Republican column has been limited still further as a result, especially as Ronald Reagan's powerful personal appeal will begin to fade from memory. Their concern is the manifestation of political conservatism in the garb of Christian fundamentalism, an important element of the Republican coalition in many parts of the country. As they have rallied in favor of school prayer and against abortion, evangelical leaders of all stripes have also loudly proclaimed that the United States must help maintain Israel's safety and military superiority.

Their reasoning, or at least their rhetoric for this come-lately Zionism, is straightforward. The simple sense of U.S. security demands it. The battle against Communist expansion demands it. But most important of all, God and Scripture demand it. In the words of one veteran Zionist leader: "Jimmy Swaggert says things on national television that my rabbi wouldn't say in his living room!"

In the justifiable enthusiasm to cultivate friends in any corner, Israeli leaders, both in Jerusalem and throughout the United States, have actively encouraged links between America's Jews and Evangelicals. They have shared the podium with them, encouraged tourism and financial investment among them, and offered them coveted awards. Though not without some misgivings, U.S. Jewish leaders have followed suit and at times overtaken their mentors in both passion and enthusiasm.

The advantages of fostering a friendship with a well-organized and politically favored community of substantial size and resource are evident. But the development has troubled many U.S. Jews, leaders and rank-in-file among them. Because of their distance, these are concerns that Israelis will not fully appreciate.

First, Zionism implies the renaissance of Jewish identity in its ancestral homeland. U.S. Jews' political directions, at least in part, are based on their perceptions of support for the well-being of that homeland and the people attached to it. There is something monumentally inappropriate, even ironic, about joining forces with those whose theo-

logical foundations call for damnation in its most literal sense to all
who fail to reject other religious beliefs and who do not choose salvation through Jesus. To join in political coalition with evangelical
Christianity is at best an anathema.

In fact, fundamentalist theology is so close to the surface of its
political organizations that it has emerged in honest, though ill-con-
ceived, public discourse. Pronouncements regarding the aural capaci-
ties of the Deity, whose prayers he hears and whose he does not, stand
as obvious cases in point. Embarrassing though they may be, such
comments are rarely retracted, for honesty cannot be recanted. One
who accepts unequivocally the evangelical Christian call must have
difficulty tolerating those who reject not just its fundamentalism, but
its very Christianity.

Of course, it is precisely this call that informs Evangelicals' support
for Israel; convictions about U.S. security or long-standing moral
commitments are only secondary. Put graphically, the Second Coming
requires that Jews be gathered in their land so that they may accept
Jesus in the way that they rejected him in times past. Zionism has
been turned on its head.

Add to this a missionary zeal that cannot be denied. The titles and
organizational manifestations are numerous: Messianic Judaism, Hebrew Christians, Bnai Sar Shalom, Bnai Yeshua, or Jews for Jesus.
By whatever name, fundamentalist proselytizing among Jews, giving
witness to the divinity of Jesus and to the infidelity of those who reject
him, has become a scourge and a plague, particularly, though not exclusively, among Jewish youth.

These more recent forms have a particularly insidious character.
Whether as a genuine expression of religious fervor or merely a cynical ruse, the liturgy and the ritual of many services are remarkably
similar to practices in traditional Jewish homes and houses of worship.
Many estranged Jews are vulnerable to such appeals. The classic image is the college student with minimal Jewish education who is far
from home, seeking friendship and a familiar environment. It is an
image that at times includes faculty and staff on campuses as well.
The appeal has also taken hold among newly arrived Russian or Israeli
immigrants, too ignorant or indifferent to know much better. It has
also been leveled at elderly Jews seeking companionship and an inexpensive hot meal. This is a ministry that reaches more than simply the
youth.

The present discussion would be no more than a harangue but for a gnawing sense that political and theological expressions of Christian fundamentalism are not isolated phenomena. Both logic and experience imply that the overarching evangelical priority, one that cements all others, is the call to spread the gospel, especially among Jews. Is it too cynical to suggest that large fundamentalist political organizations, the Moral Majority or the Religious Roundtable as examples, are supporting well-heeled missionary movements even as they proclaim their allegiance to Israel's security—and that their support is more than just moral?

Finally, a newfound alliance between Jewish voters and the forces of the political and religious right may also be poor politics. At the very least, it can put the U.S. Jewish community in rather ticklish and embarrassing circumstances. The past few congressional elections make the point painfully clear. Conservative candidates have ridden the coattails of the popular mood, gaining control of the Senate and making major inroads in the House of Representatives, the 1986 congressional elections notwithstanding.

Yet, despite what has been offered as a change in the context of U.S. liberalism, Israel still has many close Democratic friends in Congress, friends whose primary political sins are their long-standing liberal commitments. Some, like Paul Sarbanes, were threatened by this new conservatism. Others, like Frank Church or Birch Bayh, were defeated by candidates whose conservative credentials were impeccable but whose declared concern for Israel was unproven at best. Even if political support is by its nature selective and eclectic, an alliance with Republican and conservative resurgence may be contrary to simple political sense.

With it all, the change in political mood, the noted conservative shift, may only be temporary and short-lived. As with most political contests, presidential elections are frequently won because of the appeal of a single individual. His ability to capture the vote is often based on little more than media presence.

Ronald Reagan's coattails have been remarkably short. Perhaps the Republican electoral conquests of 1980 and 1984 were little more than personal victories that imply no grand political realignment. Indeed, as of November 1986, control of the Senate has swung back to the Democratic party where it resided for decades. The new conservatism and its swipe at the Jewish electorate is likely to loom ever more distant as Reagan retires from the scene.

As a result, Jews will continue to favor liberalism and the Democratic party. But will the reverse be true, that is, will liberalism favor them? Or will it continue to estrange them, take them for granted, and assume that they have no political choice? It remains for the Democratic leadership to rethink the needs of all its middle-class minorities lest it become a captive to the rainbow coalition and the forces of Jackson and Farrakhan. The reevaluation must come soon, before Jewish voters, as an example, take the choices available to them much more seriously.

PART TWO

Israel: The Promised Land

5

Haredim and Emunim: Religious Extremism and Israeli Life

I

I approach the old neighborhood from the bus stop on the main street. The road sits on a steep decline filled with potholes. The simple stone houses are necessarily built at a slant. They form a random pattern along the sidewalk, with very few more than one story high. It's all in sharp contrast to the more modern structures in the center of town. But in Jerusalem, contrast is a way of life.

More jarring is the contrast in human architecture. Except for the occasional tourist or visitor, the men are dressed in traditional Hasidic garb. Black hats and long black coats are the uniform, matched to white shirts with no ties. Conformity is the order of the day.

The women also dress modestly in the extreme. They eschew modern fashion, wearing long drab clothes reminiscent of another era, and they shave or cover their heads at all times. The result is nothing less than unattractive, and I suppose that is its intent.

Women play classic roles as mothers and housewives here. They raise large families and spend much time shopping and cooking. In addition, some work outside the home, sewing or operating small tourist shops, but by no means does this liberate them. Since they are probably supporting husbands devoting all their time to religious study, their work merely reinforces the status quo and ties them still further to the ways of tradition. That tradition dictates male dominance in their lives.

How different they all are from the Western images on the main streets of the city. There, young men parade in tank tops and designer jeans, their women in leather slacks and a tangle of chains or imitation jewelry. What ever else is said about Israel's youth, tradition and modesty do not define them.

In reaction to this characteristic, there are warnings scrawled on the uneven walls of the buildings here. They enjoin visiting females to dress appropriately while negotiating the narrow streets of Meah Shearim. It's been said that zealous teenagers have dropped tar or honey on passersby who do not meet their standards of religious modesty.

Of course, many societies have their religious fringe, people who live reclusively at the edge of society, but those of Meah Shearim and others of like mind in Israel are not quiet, retiring sorts. Their political beliefs are scrawled in black paint all over their walls.

"Judaism and Zionism are mutually exclusive!" read the bold letters in clearly American script. The message is unmistakable. For the residents of Meah Shearim, the creation of a Jewish state in Israel was more than a mistake, it was a sin, a crime, a usurpation for which the Jewish people will forever pay. To cooperate with it is ungodly collaboration.

I walk down the broad stone steps and into what passes for a marketplace. From above I hear the voices of children at study as they recite their lessons. I hear Biblical verses chanted in the singsong fashion that has characterized such study for a millenium. I look at them through the window.

This square is the center for a group that calls itself Neturei Karta. Loosely translated, it means guardians of the city, a Talmudic reference to the sages and scholars of a town. But they are not just innocent young school children immersed in religious study.

I have now arrived at the home of a fiery old gentleman, reputed to be one of the early ideologues of this movement. Reb Chaim, they call him, respectfully and with deference. Though retired from the fierce battles that marked his youth, he still stands as the intellectual father of many who now take his place.

I climb the steps and enter a large room filled with raw wooden tables and benches. He is hard at work cutting and sewing a black chunk of leather. Reb Chaim is a *batim-macher*, one who tools and cuts leather for *tefillin*, religious implements used during the morning prayers. His is a fine and fading art. There are few young men to replace him and few places where they can be trained.

I smile, but he barely recognizes my arrival. We did have an appointment. He motions me to sit and I do. "So you want to talk about Neturei Karta," he says to me, his long face framed by a thick graying beard, obligatory in these parts. "Hah!" he says with gusto. "He wants to talk about Neturei Karta." A pause and then, "Hah!" again.

He goes on with his cutting, and I begin to wonder if we will ever talk. Then he looks up at me, sets his tools aside for the moment and heaves a deep sigh. I sense that we are about to begin. So this is what it's like to sit at the feet of a guru, I muse.

"There is no such thing as Neturei Karta anymore." He says sharply. I look at him quizzically. "A bunch of kids who throw stones at a bus driver—you think that's Neturei Karta?" I shrug. "They take out an ad in the *New York Times* and they get their faces on the filthy television, that's Neturei Karta?"

He sighs again and returns to his tools. But this time he talks as he works. It's as if he is trying to distract himself from unpleasant thoughts. "We were Neturei Karta. We had a mission. We studied. Our thinking came from that. We were linked to the simple beauty of the past. Not today."

I nod as if I understand, but really I don't. "Today they are like robots. They yell, they chant, they hurl rocks and curses. They don't know what they are doing. It's exciting; it's been sanctioned by someone. They don't know what they are doing, or why. That's not Neturei Karta."

I ask him about the violence, about the foundations of a movement that appears to reject reality. He stares at me. "Reject reality?" he says, almost spitting the words at me. "We see evil, we speak out against it, and you say that we reject reality? Believe me, this Zionism of yours is not reality. It is a passing phase, and we will help it pass."

After a while, he speaks again. But then his words are no longer part of a conversation. They become a discourse. "I said that this is not Neturei Karta, that there is no more Neturei Karta except when strangers like you come to call. But there is also no more Zionism. The whole battle is over—dead and buried."

I began to debate the point but he stops me flat. "You think, this what we have today is Zionism?" he says. "Nonsense! It's a vestige, a dinosaur. What we have today is the child's play of old European Jews who enjoy vying for the spoils of political office. It's their game, their toy. And maybe that's the point," he says with a faint smile. "Today we have no Neturei Karta because today we also have no Zionism."

But what of the stonings, the bus stop burnings, the demonstrations, and the threats? I ask. If the movements are dead, then why the confrontation? "It is the remnant of Zionism that we battle now. This is all a passing phase; all movements of sin and iniquity must fade in contrast to our eternal values. And this wicked nationalism is not, you hear me, not part of Judaism."

I can see that it is pointless to argue, even to question him, so I give him his head. Listen:

"The Zionist heresy has robbed Judaism of its essence. We are no longer the people of the book: pacific, transcendent. Today, the world— even our own Jewish children—look to Eastern faiths, that nonsense, for their inspiration. Zionism robs us of our mission in the world."

He looks away with disgust. "What does the world know of the purity of our lives, the beauty of our Torah? Do they think of the simple Jew who for thousands of years rose with the sun to recite his Psalms—who left his life, his existence in the hands of our Creator?" A pause, a frown, and then in a rising crescendo: "No, no, no! Today when they think of us they think of guns and tanks and missiles. Today Jewish children don't learn Talmud. They learn the Middle East from the radio; they think that's Jewish. That's what your Zionism has done to us."

Now he's shouting. "Delve into the essence of Judaism and you see the bankruptcy of Zionism. It has abandoned the love of Zion, of our homeland, the love that you see in Yehuda Halevi, or the Jews of Yemen, or the mystics of Tsefaus. Look," a bit more calmly now, "our strength is that we have always rejected numbers and physical power. We choose the moral perfection of the few, not the strength of many. God will shield us with his might. That's what we believe!"

And then, as his long face turns the color of the beet, he pounds on the table. "Zionism has taken Jews and made gentiles out of them!" he bellows. Our meeting is over.

On my way back, I notice a bit of graffiti that eluded me before. "Touch not my anointed one," it reads in Hebrew, "and do no evil to my prophets.'' I recognize it as a verse from the Psalms. But in context it serves as a warning to the nations of the world that the Lord will protect his people, that they'd best not harm God's chosen who dwell in their midst.

These pietists see themselves as the chosen of the Lord. Israel is no different than any other nation that has hosted the faithful during their sojourn through history. In Reb Chaim's words: ''Zionism has taken Jews and made gentiles out of them.''

II

Religious opposition to Jewish nationalism has been part of the political and social landscape since the founding of Zionism. The creation of the State of Israel almost forty years ago did little to diffuse that opposition. On the contrary, it renewed its focus and direction.

The issue is complex. Many leaders of the devout in Eastern Europe feared the emergence of Zionism at the end of the nineteenth century. They saw in it a usurpation of divine prerogative that would alienate the faithful from their spiritual core. It was an abomination, a heresy that could never bring the salvation it promised. To be sure, love of the land of Israel was inherent in their theology. After all, hadn't the faithful prayed for a return to Zion over the centuries? But that would come with the arrival of the Messiah, literally, God's anointed one.

This business of a self-initiated restoration, of mere mortals trying to hasten the Lord's good time, had no precedent in Jewish history. It was little different from the mystical aberrations of the Middle Ages, and its adherents would do well to recall the aftermath of that experience. There the downtrodden—and even the sophisticated—followed false messiahs down the most corrupt of paths.

Anyway, they reasoned, one look at Zionist leadership should be enough to convince even the most naive observer that this was not what the Lord had wrought. Surely, if God chose to renew the Jewish commonwealth at this time, it would be founded upon ritually correct and religious effort. And the movement would be led and directed by scholars and saints.

But the nationalists were another sort. They counted secularists and freethinkers among them, people who were no less influenced by European liberalism than anything peculiarly Jewish. That such people could be involved, even unwittingly, in a task that was religious in its essence was unacceptable. On the contrary, their leadership and their participation gave testimony to the repugnance of the entire enterprise.

A good deal of their thinking is also associated with an obscure talmudic reference.* The Lord is said to have enforced a unique bargain between the peoples of the world and the Jewish nation. Apparently, the nations were enjoined "not to oppress Israel too much" during their millenial Diaspora. In return, the Lord demanded of Jews that they must not return en masse to the Holy Land and that they be loyal to the lands of their residence, never attempting to hasten the Divine Redemption.

Now this particular talmudic reference is only one homily among thousands. There is no reason to give it precedence. Nor is it any secret that the nations of the world never kept their end of the bargain. The past two thousand years of Jewish history are a catalogue of pain, brutality, and dislocation. The point doesn't phase these pietists. Their leaders have taken this singular reference and built a theology upon it. For their faithful, it has become a religious and political raison d'être, which goes a long way in explaining how Jews can live in Israel but not be of Israel.

Today these people go by several titles. The English-speaking media, both foreign and domestic, variously refer to them as ultraorthodox, zealots, or Hasidim. The Arab media has called them courageous rabbis who recognize the genuine nature of the Zionist entity. By their own terms they are Haredim, literally those who stand in awe, presumably of the power of the Almighty.

Of course, those closest to them recognize that they are not a unitary social group following the direction of one leadership. On the contrary, they are a microcosm of the mix of early religious communities in Jerusalem. Still, Haredim today are popularly lumped as one and are best known by the actions of their more radical elements. Most recently, they have gained notoriety for attacks on bus shelters that carry large advertisements for revealing swimwear. Members of the

---

*Ketubot 111a ff. By contrast, a group of scholars associated with Israel's more progressive and nationalist religious elements recently published a monograph offering thirteen reasons why these divine admonitions are no longer in force. Predictably, though the authors utilized classic Jewish sources and texts in making their case, their impact extends only to those who already agree with them. See S. H. Aviner, *Clarifications on the Matter of "And They Shall Not Rise as a Wall"* (in Hebrew) (Jerusalem: Noam, 1980).

Haredi community took these as an affront to their values of modesty and propriety, especially when they were found near their homes. Youthful activists among them defaced the billboards and, in many cases, burned the shelters to the ground.

These were not the worst offenses committed in the name of this brand of Judaism over the past four decades of Israel's existence. There have been riots near Haredi sections, for example, over questions of Sabbath observance. Vehicles have been stoned from the roadside, and school children have formed chains blocking construction as well as archaeological excavation.

Nor has their extremism been limited to domestic affairs. Through one or another Haredi organization, full-page ads have been placed in major international newspapers, proclaiming "Zionism and all its activities and entities the arch-enemy of the Jewish People." During the middle-1970s, in fact, Neturei Karta representatives carried on a correspondence with PLO Chairman Yassir Arafat welcoming the state proposed by the Palestine Liberation Organization. Though it was later denied, published reports suggested their willingness to serve as Jewish advisors to a Palestinian government-in-exile.*

At their quietest, Haredi communities live in isolation from the bulk of Israeli society. Residents do not serve in its army or civilian corps, nor will they utilize many of its services. Members of the community refuse to pay taxes or use instruments bearing the mark of Israel as a state, for example, stamps, public conveyances, and the like. Burning the Israeli flag has been a commonplace.

Most interesting of all, the authorities have been surprisingly tolerant of these overt and covert acts of sedition. They have exhibited condescending amusement and substantial restraint in the face of Haredi violence, and they appear undisturbed over Haredi opposition to taxation, conscription, or civic participation.

Perhaps this patience is born of a nostalgic symbolism that the authorities derive from Haredi life. For many government leaders, the community hearkens to a religious simplicity and innocence that they can summon from their own past. It recalls a lifestyle that was brutally uprooted and destroyed in Europe. So despite their militant anti-

---

*For a listing of sources and citations on these activities, see David Schnall, *Radical Dissent in Contemporary Israeli Politics: Cracks in the Wall* (New York: Praeger, 1979), chap. 8.

statism, adherents have been left much to their own devices, especially in comparison with other violent extremists.

It all came together in the case of the "bus stop commandos." Here individuals within the general public overresponded to the burning of these shelters. Tired of official indifference and the slow movement of justice, they vandalized synagogues and torched religious academies, painting swastikas and anti-Semitic slogans on the walls and courtyards. While shocking and outrageous, the actions are graphic illustrations of how much further the general public is from similar nostalgic sentiments. The backlash shook the very foundations of Israeli officialdom, religious and secular. Leaders of each variety condemned the violence on either edge of the social spectrum, setting into motion policies and procedures designed to cool tempers in both camps. While the responses have been salutary, the effects are temporary at best.

The issue extends far beyond the presence of a tiny fringe element residing in some of Jerusalem's older sections. Parts of the ideology have become infectious. Perhaps it is another reflection of the appeal that religious militance has recently displayed in various sectors of the globe: Western and Eastern, industrialized and developing, modern and traditional. In part it reflects a point developed elsewhere in this volume, the oversensitivity that contemporary Orthodoxy has displayed toward its right-wing constituencies.

The influence of Haredi ideology is evident among leaders and within institutions that avoided such thinking in the past—or relegated it to a secondary status. While extremist action is always perpetrated by the few on the fringe, tacit support, both moral and otherwise, is widespread in Israel and beyond.

Choosing to be ritually observant yet ideologically moderate has become an increasingly difficult task in Israel, as elsewhere. Religious leadership finds itself increasingly sensitive to anti-Zionist demands. It confronts the general public and the political establishment over issues that have been finessed in simpler times.

The issues are not theoretical. The secular majority deeply resents the thousands of draft exemptions that have been issued to students of various religious academies. It chafes under the feeling that Haredim are try to enforce religious coercion by pressuring the authorities to curtail public services, entertainment, and athletic exhibitions on the Sabbath and on holidays. These are, after all, activities in which the religious public rarely participates in any event.

U.S. Jewish forces have been drawn fully into the heat of battle over questions of denominational pluralism and the definition of personal status in Israel. The religious establishment has always been in the hands of Orthodoxy there, as part of an accommodation reached at the founding of the state. Marriage, divorce, conversion, and the like have been performed not just to Orthodox standards but by Orthodox personnel.

Some 90 percent of the U.S. Jewish community, however, do not adhere to Orthodoxy. Recently, these more liberal branches of Judaism have also actively recruited membership in the Holy Land. The religious response, popular and official, has been harsh and defensive, heaping insult upon the deviationists and threatening those who might be tempted to join in their worship.

The response has been equally harsh. Allegedly, there have been attempts to convince U.S. Jewish leaders to withhold financial and political support for Israel until it permits denominational parity in Jewish practice. Indeed a list of undesirable Israeli speakers and fundraisers was circulated among many U.S. congregations. Designations were based upon their personal or partisan position on matters of religious legislation.

The most troublesome of all—and the most ironically humorous— was the display over the question of who is a Jew. To be sure, the issue of personal status is certainly not a laughing matter, especially in a country that extends important privileges, including immediate citizenship, to those who carry Jewish identity. In Israel the latter has always been defined by traditional standards, that is, having a Jewish mother or being converted by classic ritual.

But Haredi elements—and those who sympathize with them, both in Israel and in the United States—felt the need to reinforce this accommodation. They moved to change the present Israeli ordinance covering personal status to include the words "conversion by Jewish law." Thus they hoped to exclude non-Orthodox conversion, which, to their mind, was ipso facto contrary to Jewish law. It was a move that had been attempted many times before, but this was considered a particularly auspicious moment, given two developments among U.S. Jews.

One was the recent decision within Reform Judaism to accept patrilineal descent, that is, having only a Jewish father, as acceptable initiation into the community. The second was a perceived increase in conversions performed by non-Orthodox clergy in the United States, conversions whose subjects might seek to make their homes in Israel. Actually, the issue was as much symbolic as it was substantial. Reform children of Jewish fathers but not of Jewish mothers would never be accorded Jewish status by Israeli religious leaders, no matter what the language of present legislation. Further, there have always been the products of non-Orthodox conversion trickling into Israel. They were accommodated by Israeli authorities in unsensational but traditionally acceptable fashion.

The irony and the humor were reflected in two events, the one personal and the other public. The first emerged at a local interdenominational conference on another matter altogether. Over coffee, one non-Orthodox U.S. layman put it all into succinct perspective.

"The issue has really be misnamed," he said, drawing a long sip. "We know who is a Jew and we know the rituals for conversion." He smiled, a twinkle in his eye. "The question is not who is a Jew," he said emphatically, "the question is who is a rabbi!"

When the vote came to the Knesset, the move to change the language of the law was hotly debated, as is much else within those hallowed parliamentary halls. Ultimately, it was defeated, as such changes have always been since the birth of the Jewish state. As in the past, the international media reported the results in brutal detail.

With the reports came faithful excerpts from declarations of various Parliament members. The world was treated to the insights of Arab deputies of Muslim and Christian confession, Druze members of the Knesset, Communists, freethinkers, and others. Each offered his own perception regarding the theological dimensions of Israel's official definition of Jewish law. That it happened was painful. That it was faithfully recorded in the pages of the *New York Times* and the *Washington Post* was nothing less than comical.

The presence of anti-Zionist, antistatist religious extremism in Israel is only one part of the story. A much more recent phenomenon has emerged at the opposite end of the political continuum. Its impact has been the more intense for its unanticipated concentration in the years since the Yom Kippur War of 1973.

III

Kedumim stands on a hilltop but a few minute's drive from Nablus/Shechem, the largest Arab town in the West Bank territories of Judea and Samaria and within easy commuting distance to Tel Aviv. The residents here were originally housed in an army compound known as Kaddum, hence the name.

It is but another example of the Israeli decision to allow Jewish settlement near but not in areas of Arab concentration. Homes are small but attractively landscaped with gardens, tiny patios, and canopies to protect them from the sun and rain. The settlement is crossed with pathways and includes play areas for the children. It houses a *midrashah*, a conference center that serves as a forum for the ideology that helped create this village.

I sit across from Daniella in her combination dining room/salon. She is young, dark, and quite attractive. Her tiny home is spotless and well organized. There are modern appliances, tasteful pictures on the wall, and fresh flowers on her table. Despite the lack of space, she is a model homemaker. Her children are well dressed and they speak to her softly, with respect.

She turns to me with a smile. A well-educated woman, Daniella holds a graduate degree in English literature and she proudly speaks of her love for several Western authors. But the real mission in her life is her work as spokesperson for Gush Emunim, the Bloc of the Faithful, an organization whose life's blood is settlement in Judea and Samaria. When it comes to Judaism and the land of Israel, she is an unabashed mystic.

"Gush Emunim is a spontaneous awakening," she begins slowly. "It is the most updated form of Zionism. We are a generation climbing mountains forward—toward the glories of Jerusalem and the renewal of the Temple."

I look at her quizzically. Jerusalem? The Temple? But we're high in the hills of Samaria. And anyway, is this moment really so portentous? She smiles and continues.

"Jerusalem is the heart of our people, but Shechem and Hebron are its other vital organs. You need all of these to make the body work." Then her expression turns dark and a frown covers her brow. "And these little settlements," she says softly, "are only artificial replacements." Her voice trails off.

Then Daniella begins a metaphysical discourse that I couldn't comprehend then and that I grasp no better now. I had heard a good deal of Gush Emunim ideology during the course of my research. Calls for a rededication to the land and the imminence of the Messiah abound. But most of them had a heavy overlay of political pragmatism. Her thinking was more pristine. Listen:

"This was the land on which we had our communication with God. I don't fully understand the special link between our people and God," she says, matter-of-factly, "but I believe in it." She speaks evenly with a strange calm in her voice. It is a calm that is jarring when matched with the apocalyptic visions she describes.

"Shechem, for an example, is linked with the stories of Jacob and the violation of his daughter Dinah, with Joshua and the conquest of the land, the mountains of Gerizim and Eval where Jews were admonished to do good and avoid evil. It all means that there is much energy and power in this place, energy that can be released and utilized for good under our jurisdiction. The goal must be to develop it."

Her eyes wander for a moment. She seems to be surveying the land for which she and her colleagues profess such love and devotion. "I feel this power," she tells me. "I am comfortable with it and I can act on it."

The words echo those of the founders of this movement and its spiritual forebears. Rabbi Zvi Yehuda Kook, late son of Israel's beloved first chief rabbi, gave the movement its ideological underpinnings. Both through his teachings and his example the importance of the land and the crucial role Jews must play in settling it were given prominence.

"All this land is ours," he once declared, " . . . guaranteed by the word of God." Settlement, in his mind, was "the commandment that is the basis and essence of all others, that, by means of our rule, can accomplish the act of Redemption."*

So, too, the words of one of his most famous students, Rabbi Moshe Levinger, founder of the new Jewish settlements in and around Hebron. To him, settlement on these disputed territories is "a basic principle of Jewish existence and a moral foundation of the state. . . . Certain things are above democracy," he once told me. "Certain prin-

---

*Quotes here and on the next page are from David Schnall, *Beyond the Green Line: Settlements West of the Jordan* (N.Y.: Praeger, 1984), pp. 19–24.

ciples cannot be subject to democracy. Among us settlement is one of those basic moral principles.''

But the most piercing declarations were offered to me by a young settler and student of Rabbi Zvi Yehuda who, early in his activist career, chose not to be a formal spokesman for the movement. *Kedushah*, the Jewish concept of sanctity and holiness, comes in three forms, he explained to me. There is kedushah attached to the people as a corporate body, and this is something to which any Jew could aspire. Beyond that, there exists a level of sanctity attached to the Torah, the treatise that sets guidelines for Jewish living. One who identifies with the people has a model, a blueprint by which to lead his life.

For many thousands of years, Jews had to be content with only these two links in the divine triangle. But no longer. Every bit of turf, every grain of sand, every rock, and every tree in the land of Israel is imbued with the third level of kedushah, for the land itself is a gift from the Almighty.

What better time than the present to unite these three elements of sanctity? What better time than when the Lord has signaled his approval, placing them all under Jewish control within the reach of every Jew? To consider bartering them for some ephemeral promises of international diplomacy is nothing less than blasphemy.

But I did not expect such mystical theology or resolution from a young housewife. ''I feel a great burden of balancing,'' she admits. ''At times I am almost torn between my activism and the needs of my family, but all our personal needs must be accommodated to changes in our national character.''

She looks at me with an air of finality, and any doubt I may have had of her commitment or the seriousness of her purpose are dispelled once and for all. ''Please understand,'' she tells me calmly, ''my role in the movement . . . is based on the needs of our nation. The only sovereignty over these territories is Israeli, and the number one battle call is the settlement of these areas with Jews.''

IV

The Bloc of the Faithful, Gush Emunim—the very title bespeaks a singular commitment to religious belief, activism, and resolve. The organization has existed on the radical fringe of Israeli society, defying government decrees, militantly opposing police and army units, and seeking to create its own armed force. But in many ways, in its bond with the land and in political and religious calls for a national renewal, the movement speaks to the very heart of Israeli life, Zionism and the Jewish people.

Settlement on the West Bank territories began almost immediately after their conquest in the 1967 Six Day War. The government hoped to create a string of paramilitary villages to enhance the security of large population centers. But strategic considerations aside, there was a special attraction to the areas south of Jerusalem, especially for the younger members of Israel's religious Zionist community.

These were graduates of the more progressive religious academies who had served in the 1967 War. Some were present when the Old City of Jerusalem was liberated. They were among the first to reach the holiest of Jewish sites, the Western Wall of the Temple courtyard where they prayed tearfully. They watched with awe as one shrine after another fell into Israeli hands—particularly, the Tomb of Rachel in Bethlehem and the Tomb of the Patriarchs in Hebron. God had promised these lands to their forefathers, they were taught. Now he was making good on that promise.

But the real thrust for the formation of Gush Emunim awaited another bloodletting. The Yom Kippur War of 1973 was a painful and confusing experience for Israel. Though it was able to forestall an Arab victory despite early setbacks, the results of it all were inconclusive.

Israelis were accustomed to elegant, lightning victories. If nothing else, the 1973 war represented an important psychological defeat that made the details of military strategy irrelevant. The weeks following the war were filled with painful recriminations and angry accusations as political and military leaders tried to affix blame on others and distance it from themselves.

But one group stood apart. Spontaneously, the youth of the religious Zionist public, now veterans of two wars, chose to interpret the events theologically, apocalyptically. The conquests of 1967 were indeed a gift from God, they again argued. He had returned all of their ancient homeland.

But they had done little with it over six years, and there was fear that perhaps they didn't deserve it. The Yom Kippur War, therefore, was a divine test. Would the people rise to the occasion? Could they set aside their personal feeings and respond to the will of the Lord?

For these young activists, the answer was simple. What was needed to cure the ills of the nation was a commitment to settle the territories and return the people to their purpose. The idea caught hold, and a variety of organizations and initiatives were immediately undertaken.

Throughout the decade or so of its existence, Gush Emunim and its supporters have been a constant source of annoyance and embarrassment to policymakers, creating "facts on the ground," that is, faits accomplis in the territories. There have been confrontations over specific settlements, questions of adequate protection and security for the settlers, and their status in relation to local Arab villagers. With it all, the ideals of the movement, if not its specific strategies, have had strong support among various constituencies, and it has always had articulate spokespeople at the very center of Israeli government.

Over the past two years, however, the relationships have turned a dramatic, controversial, and violent corner. Evidence has emerged suggesting a terrorist underground, a *machteret* in Hebrew, among settlers and students on the territories. Ensuing trials have shocked the nation as they implicate children of distinguished families and institutions within Israel's nationalist religious community.

They have been charged, and in some cases convicted, of car bombings that crippled the Arab mayors of large West Bank cities. They are alleged to have attacked an Islamic college in Hebron with machine guns and grenades. A conspiracy to bomb the el-Aqsa Mosque and the Dome of the Rock on the Temple Mount in Jerusalem has been uncovered, and an Arab commuter bus was attacked on its way out of Jerusalem.

Those who were genuinely appalled—or who had a vested interest in using the event to attack settlement policies—were quick to distance themselves from the accused. To them it was another example of the moral decay that naturally results when religious and messianic ramblings are given their way. A litany of ills, they warned, would befall the nation if the dangerous tendency were not aborted.

Others were more circumspect. They suggested that the violence was a spontaneous reaction to the frustrations that these people feel. They have come to expect and accept Arab animosity. Indeed, many seem to enjoy flouting it, but the unwillingness of their own government to take resolute action, whether in defense or initiative, is unforgiveable.

As graduates of the Zionist religious academies and youth organizations and as veterans of the Israel Defense Forces, members of the machteret have been raised in an ideological environment untroubled by thoughts of diplomatic or political compromise that may have moved their elders. They reject government action, as well as inaction, that does not fulfill the higher goals of Zionism and Judaism, as they perceive them.

The actions inform their response to those on the religious right. By this additional *mitzvah*, the commandment to settle, they differentiate themselves from the Haredim. This is what makes them special to the Lord, and with this they intend to leave their mark.

Actually, the existence of a militant religious and nationalist fringe may have served recent administrations. What the government favored but could not do on its own might be accomplished by these unofficial activists, with security forces standing by in restraint. Having them there also helped them to withstand external pressures at the diplomatic pork barrel. "Perhaps concessions are possible," they could argue, "but we must consider these radicals. No telling what they might do." Still, nobody ever thought that they really would.

The events also resulted in an important backlash. The public generally and the religious community particularly have been shaken by these arrests. Some of the most righteous elements of Israeli society stand accused of heinous crimes. The disdain might extend to the mission that spawned them. Is this the result of religious study? ask those who are none too well disposed toward ritual observance in any event. Is this what comes of Torah Zionism? It would be ironic indeed if the very goal of settlement is undermined and besmirched by its most adamant and militant supporters.

IV

Israelis have long lived with a tension between their broad secular majority and their staunchly religious minority. For much of their history, a modus operandi has been effectuated between government administration and religious authority. In return for civil calm and acquiesence in areas of diplomacy or economics, the religious authorities have been ceded matters of ritual and personal status. But the inherent contradictions never faded. They have often irked the majority who must live with the consequences of this unwritten truce. More than once the tensions have erupted into violent confrontations that, to some, are akin to a Kulturkampf in the making. Just as often, the tensions have been eased, if only in response to a common, external foe.

Among Haredim, this tension reflects their opposition to all of Jewish statehood. They glorify the uncanny survival of Jewish life through two thousand years of dispersion, not the ungodly innovations of the past few decades. For these pietists, simple faith, pacifism, and divine grace are the core of Jewish existence until the Lord brings the Divine Redemption, in his own good time. Jews have agreed to abstain from national agitation under oath, and those who violate the agreement will bring only sorrow and destruction.

There is a secondary focus for their militancy. They see Israeli social values as corrupting, gentile influences, lurid and degenerate. At the very least, they must be driven from areas frequented by the Haredi community. The purveyors of this sinful culture will undoubtedly pay for their crimes.

For its part, Gush Emunim and the various nationalist groups that support its agenda have glorified the classical values of modern Zionism: self-reliance, independence, and autonomy. The State of Israel, born from the ashes of the Holocaust, is itself an indication that the Divine Redemption is at hand. That parts of the homeland, formerly under foreign control, have fallen to Israeli jurisdiction is a sign from on high. The Jewish people must hasten the Redemption by simply holding fast.

For both groups, the objectives are important enough to justify violence—toward Arab neighbors, toward public property, even toward other Jews. But Haredim and Emunim alike have written off those who disagree with them as corrupt, invalid, ungodly, even seditious. This is a special quality of extremism that absolves it from the discomfort of responding to its detractors. Indeed, it is intriguing that both forces—antinationalist and pronationalist—can reach back to the same religious tradition and justify their militance and radicalism.

Some have likened the phenomenon to fundamentalist religious militance elsewhere, and indeed there are important similarities. For the Haredim, those who display gentile attitudes, dress, and behavior must be vigorously—even physically—chastened. They have abandoned the pristine values of native culture and ritual. It is a point that would warm the Ayatollah's heart.

For Gush Emunim, those who question the propriety of aggressive nationalism cannot be among God's chosen. It is the Lord who ordains ownership of the land, and that ownership must be reinforced by government action as well as by individual initiative. For both, there is a strain of xenophobia that makes all foreign influence suspect, no matter what the source, the result, or the application. The Moral Majority could easily subscribe to the position.

There are also important aspects to this particular brand of extremism that make the analogies inappropriate. Unlike both Islamic and Christian fundamentalism, neither Emunim nor Haredim have it in their power to overtake the political system. Gush Emunim is much more akin to a single-issue interest group prepared to stand for office, lobby, and generally work well within the political system. The Haredim, by contrast, have few if any overtly partisan motivations at all, though some have attempted to marshal their support for political ends.

The Ayatollah's agenda was forged in blood, both inside and outside of Iran. There is a glorification of martyrdom and an official willingness to sacrifice old men and young children on behalf of the cause. However, much of the violence attributable to both Haredi life or to the religious settlers is limited to the fringes within each group, and it is seen even by them as only one strategy to be applied in the final resort.

The most important differences of all make the Israeli brand of religious militance generic to itself. Rather than reinterpret or paraphrase, it is worth reflecting on it from the words of those cited above.

First from Reb Chaim: "Look, what do we want, after all? We want only for them to leave us alone. Let us live our lives quietly, as we did before 1948. Tell your Zionists to keep their ungodly influences away from us.

"Why is that so difficult? Must the buses run right near our homes before the end of the Sabbath? Must the filthy movies or naked women be brandished in our very faces? If they can't live a proper life, then just let us live ours!"

And then from a settler, on a lonely, windy hilltop in Samaria: "If I had my way, I would like to have only Jews living here. And that's not because I'm anti-Arab, you understand. It's because I'm pro-Jewish. Yes, if I had the physical possibility of affording my Arab neighbors to leave, I would do so.

"But with all this, if my Arab neighbors want to live at peace with me, not to uproot me or my right to live here, then fine, let's live together. It's not the optimum, but for now, I have to allow it."

6

Settlers from the New World

I

"The fact that there was a political debate over the future of Judea and Samaria, if anything, reinforced our desire to live here." Alvin is a U.S.-born settler who came to Israel about twelve years ago, with his wife and two little ones. He holds a graduate degree in psychology and now has five children. "The only defensible reason why Jews are anywhere in Israel—not just here—is a religious one. If this is not readily apparent to the world, then we have to make it so by creating facts in the region."

His words are stern and resolute. But he also sees great aesthetic appeal in his choice of residence. "When I drive to work here, I know that there's a good chance that I will see foxes and deer cross the road. There weren't many deer in Queens. I like that, and the kids are crazy about it!"

Americans are very much in evidence throughout the West Bank. Almost everywhere I visit, there are old friends or friends of old friends. Here is the brother of a classmate and there a former member of a teen group to which I once belonged. I shared a bunk in summer camp with the secretary at that *yishuv*, while at another there are the children

Portions of this chapter originally appeared in David Schnall, *Beyond the Green Line: Israeli Settlements West of the Jordan* (N.Y.: Praeger, 1984).

of family friends. Americans seem to be everywhere among the Jewish settlers of Judea and Samaria, and there are even some settlements that have been reserved for immigrants from the United States alone.

The substantial presence of these foreign-born settlers is a bit embarrassing for Israeli officialdom. How can they claim that the region is vital to Israeli security, or that it is an inseparable part of the national homeland, when many of those who choose to live there are not natives? Of course, they talk about the basic peoplehood of Jews everywhere, but these points are hard pressed unless one is already a believer. Small wonder then, that the Jewish Agency admits only to a U.S.-born population of 10 percent in Judea and Samaria.

Independent figures are hard to come by, but a Hebrew University study of ten large settlements is interesting. In only two cases did those born in the West, that is, Europe or the United States, constitute less than 15 percent. The overall average was 36 percent, and some were as high as 86 percent.* Of course, there are many different ways to calculate these data. Suffice it to say that observations and interviews certainly suggest a disproportionate number of Western—especially U.S.—settlers in Judea and Samaria. In addition, their frequent appearance in the local press and foreign media and their service as spokespeople within the movement make them visible even beyond their numbers.

I will concede a simultaneous sense of fascination and discomfort in dealing with these friends and cohorts. In a way, I can understand their motivations and even muster grudging sympathy, for we are much alike. Fulfilled are the aspirations, ingrained in our youth. Rejected is the materialism, long reviled in sermon after sermon, from one U.S. pulpit to another. It's all so simple for them.

Many have had to overcome the opposition of family and friends, who gave solemn lip service to emigration to Israel but who never considered it seriously and who often discouraged it. Undeterred, these settlers have chosen the dangers and discomforts of Judea and Samaria over their American affluence. I find this admirable, political considerations aside. If nothing else, it reflects the strength of religious conviction in the face of personal ease.

Still, a part of me reacts with some distress, possibly for the same

*Shalom Reichman, *Non-Agricultural Jewish Settlement in Judea and Samaria* (in Hebrew) (Jerusalem: Hebrew University, 1981).

reasons. Is it a sense of guilt or envy? Is it a feeling that religious motivations have misled them? I recoil at the hypocrisy of those who inspire these young people but remain in the fleshpots of America, allaying their consciences with each successive émigré. I question the wisdom and justice of it all.

The point is driven home at a settlement in formation. On my first trek to this barren hilltop, there is nothing, save a few army tents and the omnipresent Donald Duck slide. Three larger tents serve as dining hall, synagogue, and meeting place, with eating utensils, napkins, and the like kept in drawers of a rusting file cabinet. On the periphery, smaller tends are living quarters for ten or so families, the core of this new settlement.

It is a particularly hot day in July. Most everyone wears light clothing: men in khaki shorts, women in thin dresses. But as I speak to my driver, I notice a rather inappropriate image in front of a tent a few hundred yards away. There is an American rabbi of my acquaintance in a dark suit, white shirt, tie, polished shoes, and the curious gray Homburg hat that is something of a trademark.

I amble over to say hello. He is about to lunch with a young couple whose parents are his congregants. The woman strains to set a table equal to her honored guest. She is uncomfortable with the lack of elegance that I suspect never bothered her before. She's certainly not the stereotypical Jewish princess, but she was raised to believe that a proper table is basic to entertaining. Her effort to replicate at least some of it here is little short of ludicrous.

For his part, the rabbi looks comfortable and happy. He smiles as I extend my hand in greeting. Always cordial and friendly, he retains his dignified formality all the same. I can almost hear the sermon (sermons?) that would result from this visit: the great strength of these young pioneers in the face of adversity, his desire to visit and offer them support, despite danger to his own person, and the role he played in inspiring their move.

I harbor no animosity to this particular rabbi, a fine and sincere gentleman. Yet, as I regard the image—he in his formal garb, they in their settler's clothes, the tent, the rickety aluminum table, the crumpled cloth, the paper napkins—the contrast is so stark, it is jarring. Is this what we U.S. Jews look like? Is spiritual leadership contained in words alone? What am I to make of the genuine culture clash, so apparent to me on that barren hilltop?

II

American immigrants on the West Bank are often looked upon as something different, a special curiosity. The foreign media love to interview them, quoting their most militant pronouncements (frequently out of context). They enjoy photographing them, rifle in hand, next to the barbed wire gates that surround their homes. This is contrasted to the comfortable and genteel family lives they left behind.

Israeli-born settlers and government officials also see them as unique and special. Over and over again I am told that Americans who decide to live in Israel are generally more idealistic, principled, and high minded. This, of course, makes them perfect candidates for the new yishuvim of Judea and Samaria.

Perhaps this is no more than should be expected. Native Israelis do not choose their place of residence, they are born to it. It is unreasonable to expect that they would exhibit the same kind of nationalist commitment as one who comes to Israel by choice or sacrifice. In fact, many natives make it clear that whether economically, culturally, or socially, Israel is not a desireable home for them. They prefer to live in London, Paris, New York, Los Angeles, Montreal, or most stops in between.

The point rings equally true for many immigrants to Israel from Eastern Europe or the Arab world. Of course, there are those who came to Israel out of a genuine desire to be reunited with the ancestral homeland or to live a more perfect Jewish life. But a disproportionate number sought refuge. They did not come to Israel so much out of desire but rather to run from the oppressive and anti-Semitic regimes of their birthplaces.

Many have not been shy about their preference for other lands. For example, some two-thirds of those Jews allowed to leave the Soviet Union over the past decade have not chosen Israel as their new home. Similarly, affluent Jewish immigrants from Iran, Syria, and North Africa are found in large numbers throughout Europe and in the metropolitan centers of the United States. What is more, a substantial number of those who initially did choose aliyah joined friends and family elsewhere within a short period of time. Their ideological and religious ties to Israel have not been strong or of impressive duration.

But the experience of U.S. immigrants is quite different. They were not threatened by a tyrannical regime whose ire was particularly focused upon its Jewish subjects. In fact, they are accustomed to a high degree of personal freedom, professional opportunity, and efficient service from public and private sector alike. And in this, they are joined by their analogues, emigrants to Israel from places like Canada, Western Europe, South Africa, and Australia.

Consider Dina, a young woman in her twenties, now living in Shiloh with her Israeli husband. Born to a comfortable family in Brooklyn, she came to Israel permanently upon college graduation and lived in the Sinai while it was still under Israeli control. She was married in Yamit, the main Israeli settlement there. The ceremony became a symbol of protest, attracting busloads of onlookers from all over the country. When the town was dismantled and the area turned back to Egypt, the couple moved to Shiloh.

"I was not always traditional in my attitudes and values," she explains, wisps of dark hair escaping from her beige *tich'l*. "My family was religious in its outlook, but when I was in college I saw all those people having fun, and I decided that I could do the same. I soon began questioning again, though I came back to the traditional values. I guess I decided that's what I wanted of my life."

And what was the most important value that she embraced, after this period of searching and questioning? "Zionism and love for Israel were always drummed into me by my family. I had been touring Israel since I was thirteen. I've always felt that my home is here."

She smiles wistfully and speaks of the family and friends she left behind; even in Israel, most of her friends are U.S.-born, a distinct disadvantage for her husband, who speaks little English. She says by way of conclusion, "I suppose that while my family lived in New York, I was in college preparing to live in Israel." Her choice was born of freedom and personal desire, rather than involuntary constraint or extenuating need.

In fact, the freedom and success that these migrants enjoyed elsewhere often works against them in Israel. Many come quickly to odds with the highly structured, bureaucratic, and rather blasé work ethic common there. They are not accustomed to elastic time schedules and project specifications, where most anything is subject to negotiation and renegotiation. A popular witticism contends: "The first year in Israel, the new immigrant hates the aliyah agencies, the second year he hates the government, and the third year he hates the new immigrants."

But with it all, these folks do not take for granted the everyday influences of Jewish culture and values. In Israel, Jewish festivals are genuine holidays where shops and offices close, noise abates, and traffic is diminished. Gone is the sense of being odd, in the minority, out of the mainstream, that was so much a part of their lives, "over there."

Native Israelis cannot easily appreciate these nuances. The large majority profess little concern for religious observance. They may actually see it all as a nuisance. On Sabbath and holidays, theaters are dark and basic services are not readily available in most large cities. Dietary restrictions make certain foods contraband. Personal status—whom one may marry, when, and under what circumstances—is a matter decided by distant rabbis, versed in strange and esoteric rites.

So it's not surprising to find that Americans who arrive in Israel tend to be idealistic and high minded about their new homes. They have been encouraged by the officials and functionaries who facilitated their move, leading "seed groups," offering advice, and providing services in the United States, under the indirect auspices of the Israeli government. Consequently, when an American arrives in Israel, he has been taught to expect his standard of living to fall. In return he seeks a qualitative change in the nature of his social and spiritual existence.

Naive? Unrealistic? Perhaps so. Listen to Reuben, a friend of my adolescence now living with his family in Elon Moreh: "When we first moved to Israel, we lived in a comfortable apartment in Petah Tikvah, near Tel Aviv. My father and I opened a successful business and everything was going well. Yet there was something missing from our lives. I went to work. I came home. I watched television. I might just as well have been living in Brooklyn. Now," he smiles gesturing to the line of temporary homes on this rocky hilltop in Samaria, "now I feel like I am part of something. I am building a city."

Of course the overwhelming majority of U.S. immigrants—and the overwhelming majority of Israelis—never consider settling in Judea and Samaria. But the visible representation of Americans there can, in part, be attributed to this factor. Life in Jerusalem, Tel Aviv, or Haifa may not be that different, *different enough*, from the lives they left behind. Those who are most demanding may be able to satisfy their needs best in the intimate, simple, and newly developed environs of the West Bank yishuv. Here they feel that they can make a life that will count, among people of similar outlook, values, and aspirations.

III

Not all U.S.-born settlers are marked by ideological resolve, however. Many came to live in Judea or Samaria for other reasons as well. Some see their lives in more practical, even mundane terms.

One part of it is the desire to live in a smaller, less urban environment. Evidently, many came from comfortable suburban communities prior to their emigration. They are accustomed to single-family residences with private property and breathing space, a rarity among Israel's nonagricultural elements, except among the very wealthy. They also like community patterns that encourage close ties among neighbors, greater freedom for their children, and a measure of communal activism. The impersonality of apartment living in Jerusalem, Tel Aviv, or Haifa offers little of that.

Other U.S. settlers came from the big cities of the Northeast or Midwest. For them, suburbia was part of their social aspirations, a reference for their upward mobility. Moving to Israel may have been an alternative to buying a home in Skokie, Illinois; Brookline, Massachusetts; or Silver Springs, Maryland.

Related is the desire to help develop a community from the outset and see that it conforms to certain religious and social norms. The suburban lifestyle of young, upwardly mobile Orthodoxy in the United States is a research topic in itself. For our purposes, it is fair to say that their communities are characterized by much socializing and hospitality, with great emphasis upon the young. A sense of belonging, structured by the synagogues they attend and the private schools to which they send their children, cement the relationships. These institutions are expected to provide guidelines for personal behavior, cultural and educational enrichment and further opportunities for social interaction.

Despite their desire for a fairly high level of community organization and structure, these settlers from the United States still value their own privacy and freedom. They are not well suited for experiments in socialism, communal dining halls, or restrictions on their professional pursuits and income. Most are well educated, accustomed to commuting to work, and unwilling to change their habits to facilitate some brand of cooperative agriculture or industry. Some receive financial assistance from parents and in-laws in the United States. They are not likely to share these personal gifts with friends and neighbors in the name of some social philosophy.

The Israeli response is the *yishuv kehilati* (community settlement), roughly equivalent to the incorporated village common in U.S. suburbs, but with important differences. It offers the settlers an opportunity to structure the community along familiar lines, without a level of social control or restriction that might be considered oppressive. Particularly in the newer settlements, it is an opportunity to get in "on the ground floor," that is, prior to the formation of a closed establishment and informal leadership.

But the yishuv kehilati offers something more. It is a chance to create an environment impossible in the United States: one closed to any who do not display a fairly high level of religious observance and ritual practice. In the past, these folks *had* to live near the non-Jew or the Jewish freethinker. Now that they have the choice, now that they are involved in the formation of the community itself, many seek a residence in an area limited to those at or near their own levels of religious observance. This newfound intolerance augurs ill for a country already suffering an exaggerated rift between its religious and secular elements.

Rita and Larry are both originally from Brooklyn. Today they live at Karnei Shomron, a large settlement founded in 1977. There are about 150 families at Karnei Shomron, "and only four are not religious" she tells me proudly. Most residents commute about forty-five minutes to Tel Aviv. The settlement is slated for further development along with others in its area.

"Why did we move to Samaria?" Rita asks rhetorically. She is chubby, with a bright smile and a friendly manner. Her small children run about playfully, making quite a racket as we talk. Her husband tries to quiet the two, but to little avail. We push on anyway.

"The truth is, we simply couldn't afford the prices in town, especially in Jerusalem," Larry answers. I have heard that before. A young carpenter of my acquaintance moved directly from Toronto to Kiryat Arba. His great dream was to live in Jerusalem, but he couldn't afford it. He'd save some money so that someday he could.

Rita interrupted my wandering thoughts. "When we began looking, we got interested in a yishuv. Until then we didn't even know what a settlement was or where Samaria was either!'' She smiles and gestures. It's all that simple! What's to understand about it anyway? Aren't people always changing their minds and seeking new places to live? I smile.

"But once we got involved in the whole project, I guess we caught the ideology too,'' Larry is quick to add. The couple has since been meeting with other Americans in Israel and communicating with those contemplating aliyah from the United States. Tours and information sessions have been arranged toward the goal of filling the region with Jews.

"Look,'' he tells me, perhaps a bit shy about having admitted to his pragmatism. "It's true that the political statement was secondary for us. Still, the only way to keep Samaria is to settle it. Israel should say that this land is ours and that's it. Anyone who doesn't like it can move. Otherwise, learn to live in peace!''

We speak of life on the yishuv, the joys and the difficulties they have found. Rita's parting thoughts confirm my own. "It's really not all that difficult,'' she says as I rise to leave. "Everyone is friendly and the whole place is made up of similar people.'' She explains that because it is not mixed, that is, composed of people with varying degrees of religious belief, "the settlement is more successful.'' I look at her quizzically.

Rita pauses to collect her thoughts. "When it's Shabbat, its Shabbat,'' she begins slowly. "If your kid wants to play with a neighbor, you don't have to worry about *kashruth*, you know, what he is going to eat. There is uniformity, and that's a big help.'' In the narrow range, perhaps that's true. Anyway, it's what this couple wanted.

It's also what Aaron and Leah wanted, only more so. They came to Israel from Peoria, Illinois, where he was a Hebrew school teacher. They lived for a while in a new apartment complex on the northern outskirts of Jerusalem. "When the government decided to place North African immigrant families in the same buildings,'' Aaron says plaintively, "the place became an instant slum. Honestly, it was like some bombed-out inner-city project, nothing like what we came to Israel for.'' So they moved to Maaleh Amos.

The Israelis have a name for places like Maaleh Amos. They call them black, but not because of the racial mix of residents or the color of the landscape. They call them black because of the clothes worn by virtually all the men who live there. Maaleh Amos is a yeshiva community.

It's really an interesting story. For generations, large academies of higher Jewish learning have provided living space and a small stipend for married students and their families. Known as a *kolel*, it allows them to continue their studies, despite the responsibilities of married life.

Maaleh Amos is a rather enterprising and creative response to this mission by a particular Jerusalem yeshiva. Its leaders could not secure adequate space and were unwilling to pay the oppressive costs in Jerusalem proper. They chose instead to settle these senior students, many with several young children, on the last patch of brown as one descends the Hebron Hills toward the desert and the Dead Sea.

The contrast is a striking one for me. As I approach the front gate, I am welcomed by a tall young man with a thick black beard. He is dressed in typical yeshiva garb: white shirt, no tie, black pants, *zizith*—long woolen fringes attached to the corners of a tunic-type undershirt—hanging at his sides. As he bends to lift a large metal propane cannister, the wind wreaks havoc with his *payot*, the curled hairlocks he comes behind his ears. The rest of his hair is close cropped, supporting a large, black velvet *kippah*, to differentiate from the knitted skull caps worn by the more modern settlers elsewhere.

As he walks toward me I turn in the direction of an odd thundering sound. It's a large herd of wild camels trotting by. Apparently these are his nearest neighbors. Even the local Arabs don't set up villages here. We smile and Aaron introduces me to his friend Hayim.

We walk toward his home. Along the way we pass young girls in long white socks, wearing dresses with sleeves to their knuckles. Large woolen *taliyoth*, prayer shawls, hang on the clothes lines between the caravans. All the men wear round velvet *kippot* and dark slacks. Some have dark jackets and all have thick beards. As these things go, Maaleh Amos is black as the night. Aaron smiles again.

"I'm not here for ideological or political reasons at all," he tells me. "This is simply where the yeshiva sent me. If it were on the other side of the green line [the pre-1967 Border], I'd go there. I'm seeking a particular level of *frumkeit*, a religious atmosphere—and, of course, inexpensive housing." His use of the older, Yiddish term is revealing. He does not care to identify himself with the kinds of religious commitment better known among Jewish settlers of these parts. He's just another kolel boy trying to follow the direction of his yeshiva.

His talk, his inflection, his gestures are all classically those of the traditional yeshiva student. We enter his home. It too has the familiar sights and smells of a kolel family. There are large silver candelabra for the Sabbath. The dining room has an oversized mahogany table and shelves of enormous talmudic and rabbinic folio. I feel as if I am somewhere in Brooklyn.

"I like it here," Aaron explains as I look at his books, "but life is hard. I commute each day to Jerusalem where I teach first grade. The bus leaves before 7:00 A.M. and it takes over an hour. I get back in the early afternoon and spend the day learning. I don't have a car yet and except for basic foods, everything is in Jerusalem."

I look out the window. There are paths crossing the settlement in every direction, but no green at all. "Winter is rough here," he goes on. "The rain is bad and it turns everything to mud. I'm very sensitive to the cold, and I don't do well at all. But I love the atmosphere and the kids have dozens of friends." Then he sets himself apart from yeshiva types elsewhere.

"I don't know how to use a gun yet," he tells me, "but I'm learning. It would be very foolish to travel the roads here without one. And if we do intend to get a car . . . well, it will just have to become part of my life." Along with the religious values, the talmudic tracts and the rabbinic dicta, I suppose.

One more reflection of Americans on the territories comes from Kfar Yacov (not its real name), a tiny settlement but a few kilometers east of the lush kibbutzim that constitute Israel's bread basket "on the other side." Despite the good intentions of all concerned, it is not one of the more successful settlements.

The yishuv was limited to U.S. immigrants, for fear that in a mix with Israelis, the natives would soon dominate. It was established as a *moshav*, with private homes but with corporate industry, agriculture, and control of durable goods. It is also a strictly religious community that has banned television for fear of its negative influence, much to the dismay of several families. Strains have emerged in the personal relations between members of the moshav. There are barely twenty families living there and very few newcomers on the horizon.

There I meet Jack, a former computer programmer from a Washington, D.C., suburb, who now works a vineyard in the predawn hours. Jack is very frank about his reasons for settling in the territories. "I had no intention of making a political statement," he tells me in an offhanded manner. "We chose this place because it was available. As far as I'm concerned, there is no difference between one side of the green line or the other."

He thinks for a moment, looks at the other houses around us and shrugs. "So far as I know, no one came here for ideological or political reasons. People came here because it was available!" We walk about. He proudly shows me the various public structures: a combination synagogue/meeting hall, the mikvah, the administrator's office. We talk about the rifts that have plagued this settlement since its inception. Many have had to do with levels of public religious observance. Modesty of the women's dress is a particularly sore point.

Then I ask him about the small sidearm he clutches. "It's funny," he says a bit sheepishly, almost embarrassed. "Occasionally I feel like a kid with a toy. You have a gun, it's like a toy." His voice drops. "Most of us, if we had to use it in a moment of stress, I think we probably would make in our pants." His face reddens. Then he turns away and stares at the rocky desolation that is his landscape.

"I think about that a lot," he confesses. "What would happen if, God forbid, I had to use the gun to defend myself or the people I was with? I hope I'll be able to do it. I have trust in God, though, that I'll never have to." And with that, Jack walks away. Clearly, not all Americans on the West Bank are great pioneers who come out of a sense of religious or national motivation. Nor are they all courageous defenders of their faith.

IV

By way of contrast, there are also stories of Americans who made the ultimate sacrifice on the altar of their beliefs about Judea and Samaria. An American student at Kiryat Arba, for example, was stabbed while on a day's visit to Hebron with friends. His companions foolishly pursued the attackers, leaving the victim to bleed in the streets. He was taken to an Arab hospital by local residents, where the staff could not properly identify him. He died soon thereafter. It is a gory tale.

The one I found most compelling, however, was marked by its tragic nobility. David Rosenfeld, a graduate of Georgetown University, came to Israel with his new bride, Dorit, in the fall of 1980. He was an open and friendly sort, bent on making a home for himself in Israel, where he believed all Jews should live. She was a sophisticated Manhattan woman who met her husband while both were students at Haifa University.

They lived first in Tel Aviv and later in Jerusalem. David worked at a bank and in a supermarket, but he was a free spirit who did not enjoy the noise and the rush of the city. He sought an atmosphere where he might get more closely involved with people as individuals. The couple visited Tekoah, near Bethlehem, and David was taken with this place that had been the home of the Prophet Amos, herald of justice and champion of the poor.

So the two, now with a young son, moved from the city to Tekoah. Contrary to the expectations of several neighbors, they managed nicely, despite the loneliness and hardship of life in a tiny settlement on a windy hilltop. David, in particular, enjoyed the solitude. He made communion with like-minded friends and soon became well known for his willingness to share and to help.

He also had vision. Tekoah stands in the shadow of the Herodion, an imposing structure high on a peak in the Judean wilderness. Built as King Herod's winter palace almost two thousand years ago it commands a magnificent view of the entire region. David believed that it had potential as a tourist site, providing employment and income for the local residents, Jew and Arab alike. From the rocky and barren surroundings, he would help develop a commercial success.

David became the supervisor of the Herodion. His task was to create the great national park and camping area he foresaw. He was assisted by Muhammed, a local Arab. Despite differences in their background, the two became good friends, and David took pride and satisfaction in the relationship.

On Saturday, the Jewish Sabbath, David would remain home to pray with his family while Muhammed stood in charge of operations at the Herodion. On Friday, David was alone, while Muhammed fulfilled his own religious obligations. It was a relationship built on mutual respect and trust, something all too rare in these parts.

It was on just such a Friday, in early July, that David Rosenfeld was brutally murdered. Alone and unarmed—he owned an Uzi but rarely carried it with him—his body was found in a sea of blood. The police stopped counting slash marks near one hundred; it was no longer possible to distinguish one from the other. They did note that the majority of the wounds were inflicted in the victim's back.

Investigators did not have to look very hard to find the killers. A trail of blood led David's friends and neighbors to two Arab teenagers who confessed quickly. Further inquiry led to a gang of terrorists, with an impressive arsenal of weapons and explosives. Rumors linked the mob to a local Arab notable, although no firm evidence emerged.

As is common in such circumstances, the homes of the murderers were destroyed by Israeli security forces and left in a pile of rubble, as much a memorial to David Rosenfeld as a reminder to others with aspirations of brutality and bloodshed. But the response of the settlers of Tekoah deserves mention.

There were some, a bare few, who reacted with fear. Might there be reprisals? They conjured a horrifying image of angry Arab villagers attacking their settlement and driving them from their homes. Some talked of evacuating their families or spending a few days elsewhere.

A larger group reacted in the opposite manner. Why wait for a trial, the slow movement of justice in a democratic system? Why not confront these terrorists and drive them from the area? Let's teach them that innocent Jewish blood will not go unavenged and unredeemed. Let's do to them, they reasoned, what they would probably like to do to us!

But cooler heads prevailed over both groups. Instead of retreating in fear or advancing in attack, the group assumed what they considered to be the "proper Zionist response." What better tribute to poor David Rosenfeld than to found another yishuv in his memory? How better to demonstrate that acts of violence and terror will neither drive Jews from the territory nor lead them to condone a bloody response? Simply create a new settlement for each comrade whose life is stolen.

So they founded El-David, named for Eli Pressman, another Tekoan who had fallen in Lebanon, and for David Rosenfeld. The yishuv was hurriedly set up with tents and caravans. Appropriate to its namesake, it stood on the foothills of the Herodion. Ironically, the land acquired was no more than a few hundred yards from the pile of rubble that once was the house of David Rosenfeld's murderer.

Not all incidents of violence on the West Bank are treated with such

chivalry. This one was exemplary. The story is but one illustration of
the ideals and principles often attributed to U.S. immigrants who find
their way to settlement in Israel's new territories, beyond the green
line.*

*Aside from interviews with friends and neighbors at Tekoah, the foregoing was
culled from reports in the *Jerusalem Post* (July 12, 1982) and the special feature by
Israel Amrani, "David's Dream" *Jerusalem Post*, August 4, 1982.

7

The Insoluble Dilemma

I

Arab life on the West Bank is marked by contrasts, some so dizzying that they confuse even the most astute observer. Wealthy merchants who live in grand homes and dress in distinctly Western style drive their big cars past poor villagers living in shacks subsidized by the United States through the United Nations. There are modern college-educated professionals and journalists and there are peasants who sell cactus fruit and grapes on the roadside.

A devout Muslim hajji walks the streets of Hebron in traditional garb, while Christians pray at the Basilica of the Nativity in Bethlehem and agnostics in Nablus hold sacred only the writings of Marx and Lenin. There are conservative farmers and business people whose children attend local schools and study militancy and radicalism from homegrown intellectuals.

In many ways the contrasts reflect the political and social history of these parts over the past several decades. Residents of this territory have been tossed by countervailing winds, each reinforcing tendencies that were already there. Influence in their world has always been based on family and village affiliations, property and personal contacts. These patterns have had to contend with turbulent changes and international upheaval.

Under Jordanian rule, West Bank residents were not encouraged to become politically active, much less consider self-determination or autonomy. The focuses of political leadership were the mayors of the larger cities, who were appointed functionaries of the Jordanian government and who could be summarily dismissed at the pleasure of the crown. In addition, most influential West Bank families had links with commercial interests on the other side of the Jordan. This also encouraged conservative, pragmatic politics.

The Israeli conquests of 1967 created confusion and disorientation. Was steadfast opposition toward this new ruler the appropriate response, or could these new circumstances also offer new opportunities for negotiated freedom and independence? Would moderation yield the best results, or should one of the calls to militance and radicalism be embraced? If so, which one?

Change opened the door to conflicting political trends that have existed in the Arab world since it began its flirtation with modernity about a century ago. The West Bank resident could survey the political field and have his choice of several options, each with its inherent benefits and risks.

For example, he could continue to claim allegiance to Jordan. After all, there were many from his area who had held positions of importance in the Jordanian parliament. Some even rose to cabinet posts. He had friends and relatives in Amman, and many neighbors had left their homes to seek refuge there. It was a natural affiliation.

But what had Jordan done for him since 1948? Economic and social development was low; disease and illiteracy were high. Opposition parties were banned, and most who dared to speak out were imprisoned. Sure, he had friends and relatives on the other side of the river, but many of them were living in refugee camps under conditions as bad as any he knew.

Then there were calls to pan-Arabism. All Arabs are one, they claimed. Forget the national boundaries that have been created throughout the Arab world. These are merely vestiges of British or French imperialism. The Lebanese Maronite, the Saudi Imam, the Libyan socialist—they are all brothers united by centuries of history, language, and culture. To retain artificial divisions plays into the hands of those who seek to subjugate the region. West Bank Arabs were invited to join in a movement of cultural and supranational liberation.

But these claims were also suspect. Beyond rhetoric, the Arab world had done little to help those they called brothers on the West Bank.

Egypt and Syria both coveted the territory and offered no real indication that they cared for the social and economic well-being of its residents. Jordan unilaterally annexed the area over the objections of every other Arab state, and the oil-rich sheikhs of the Persian Gulf just sat on their hands.

In the Arab world, the Palestinian—whether he lives on the West Bank, in Jordan, in Lebanon, or elsewhere—is something of a pariah. He is more cosmopolitan and better educated than the bedouin or the desert nomad, and therefore he is always the outsider. Most Arab states are sectarian conglomerations with shaky leadership based on personal or family networks. The presence of a large refugee population could tip a delicate balance and ignite tensions. No, pan-Arabism was not an option for Arabs on the West Bank.

In fact, most chose one of three other paths. The largest by far remained apolitical. Whether out of ignorance, indifference, or simple good sense, they looked at the whole affair with amused detachment. The Israeli conquest of 1967 really needn't change their lives that much. Day to day, the struggle was still to eke out a living, maintain authority over the family, and retain local status in the villages where most of them lived.

To this day, a casual visitor is impressed with the traditional, almost pastoral lifestyle that seems to characterize most of the local population. The image is very different from the assumption of radicalism generally attached to these people. It's almost as though a change in the status of the land really doesn't affect the life of its residents. Perhaps it is so with most of the world's population.

A parallel decision was made by many local notables to continue their pragmatic political and economic activities after 1967, as they had for generations. If cooperating with the new Israeli authorities meant that sewage and sanitation services would be improved or that there would be more money for roads and schools, then so be it. There was no disloyalty implied, simply a desire to go on with life, to retain traditional social structures and authority patterns under a changed jurisdiction.

As a result, many of the older, well-established leaders resigned themselves to cooperate with Israel on matters of day-to-day administration. For their part, the Israelis demanded little. Jordanian currency remained legal tender, children studied from most of the same schoolbooks, and religious courts mediated by the same standards as under

Jordanian rule. If autonomy means discretion over purely local matters, then it has always characterized Israeli rule.

II

There was a younger element, however, for whom business as usual was inadequate. Most were from the cities where they attended local high schools and colleges and came under the influence of teachers who had no stake in the present social system. Many lived in refugee camps. Others had friends who did. They looked at local leaders with distrust and suspicion. A moderate Israeli administration could be the very target for Palestinian independence, they reasoned, something impossible under Jordanian rule. Now was not the time to consolidate traditional patterns of status and control but to create a whole new system.

For them, militant nationalism was the only route. They rallied about a new political unit known as the Palestine Liberation Organization. Created in 1964, the PLO was a relatively unimportant actor on the Middle Eastern stage when Israel took the territories. But its cry of armed resistance found a ready audience among the young. *Sumud*, steadfastness in opposition to Israeli rule, was to be their mark.

Its words were attractive to listeners who knew nothing but deprivation and political restriction. By 1967 an entire generation had grown up in or near refugee camps. They were raised with the image of a Palestinian national identity quashed by Zionist aggression. Most had friends or relatives who lived under squalid conditions in Jordan or southern Lebanon but who remembered their Palestinian homeland. Ironically, the Israeli victory of 1967 helped activate these elements behind the PLO.

The more radical the PLO could portray itself, the more attractive it became. And the more attractive it became, the more unacceptable it was to the Israelis. Their hard-line refusal to meet with the PLO, in turn, only raised its stock among its supporters. The PLO soon won the endorsement of the Arab world.

There were numerous social and political organizations on the territories, each claiming to speak for the Palestinians, but in October of 1974, the Arab League, meeting in Rabat, invested the PLO as the "sole legitimate representative" of the Palestinian people. In a swipe at Jordan, it denied individual Arab nations the right to speak for the

Palestinians and all but granted head-of-state status to PLO chief, Yassir Arafat.

The PLO was buoyed still further when Arafat was invited to address the United Nations just a few weeks later. Carrying a pistol and donning his rebel garb, he called for the creation of a secular democratic state in Palestine. The words were readily accepted not only in the Middle East but in many of the world's capitals. Within a year, the United Nations passed a resolution equating Zionism with racism. Soon the PLO was formally recognized by governments in Europe and the Third World.

Still aside from the popularity and legitimacy accorded the PLO at home and abroad, its hold on Arab politics was rooted elsewhere. As the official representative of the Palestinian people within the Arab world, it was the beneficiary of huge sums of money from several Arab governments.

For example, in 1978 an Arab summit was convened in reaction to the peace initiatives. To signal their rejection, the assembled created a special fund to support PLO efforts and subsidize West Bank militance. A direct grant of $250 million was to be provided annually to the PLO. An additional $150 million was to be distributed annually to promote sumud among the inhabitants of the territories. Part of these funds would be funneled through a joint PLO-Jordanian committee. The rest would be placed at the sole discretion of the PLO.

Needless to say, the funds were not distributed randomly. The PLO has rewarded its supporters in direct relation to their intransigence. Since its best recruits tend to come from the squalor of the refugee camps, alleviating social ills would run counter to its revolutionary aims. In a very real sense, the worse it gets, the better it gets.

In addition, the PLO developed independent sources of income from investments, arms sales, shipping, and other commercial enterprises as well as guerrilla training. The Israeli invasion of southern Lebanon uncovered a financial empire held together by terror and intrigue. The PLO controlled Lebanese ports in Tyre, Sidon, and Tripoli. It had extensive holdings in hashish and had united several dozen individual businesses under a single corporation known as Zamed. At its height, it employed a workforce of over five thousand. As a result, the PLO was able to reward West Bank supporters handsomely. Particularly in the bigger towns, it provided large subsidies for young leaders and students who opposed the traditional elites. They called for strikes and demonstrations against Israeli authorities and reviled those who preached moderation.

Older leaders were challenged to equal the zeal of these young militants. The PLO's huge financial resources helped tip the balance in its favor and quiet any opposition. Once the mayoral offices were captured, influencing the local citizenry through patronage, favors, and cash was a relatively easy task.

There was also the corollary. If the PLO had ample resources to inspire support for radicalism, it was not shy about issuing sanctions against those who suggested that moderate means could better serve the interests of West Bank residents. First, warnings were issued in characteristic Arab fashion. Where personal status and political connection are basic to social standing, the organization set to defame its targets. Moderate leaders were attacked as traitors and publically scorned by friends and colleagues until their credibility was worn.

Those whose opposition was more intractible and more threatening were treated less kindly. The classic example was Sheikh Huzander, the late Imam of Gaza. The sheikh was a religious leader who had tentatively declared his support for the Egypt-Israel peace treaty and the quest for a negotiated solution to the Middle East conflict. He had spent two months in Egypt with the hope of promoting Gaza as a link in the international peace process.

Upon his return home, the elderly sheikh was brutally murdered, his throat slit as he approached his doorstep returning from evening prayers. The Popular Front for the Liberation of Palestine, a militant wing of the PLO, claimed responsibility for the murder. It threatened a similar fate for anyone who collaborated with "the Zionist enemy." The sheikh had two sons who belonged to the PLO.

More recently, the PLO has fallen on difficult times. Its economic resources are still substantial, but it has been pressed by its own component parts. Always a loose confederation of extremists at best, individual groups have undertaken terrorist missions of their own in many of the capitals of Europe as well as in the air and on the high seas.

In so doing they have attracted the attention and support of particular states with an interest in competing with the PLO for its constituency or simply promoting instability, especially aimed against the West. Syria, Libya, and Iran have been identified within the Islamic world as sponsors of international terror who have bankrolled and sheltered such activity. The Soviet Union and its clients in Eastern Europe and in the Carribean have also made this terrorist connection.

Specific Western nations, notably the United States and Great Britain, have struck back selectively on both military and diplomatic fronts. Concerted efforts among the Western allies or even within the business communities of these nations have been slow and uneven, however. Revelations regarding negotiated hostage release in return for aid to Iran have called the integrity of the stance into serious question.

By contrast, Arafat himself has come under fire, both literally and figuratively, to promote greater militance and ever more daring action in opposing a Zionist presence in the Middle East. For several months in late 1983 he was besieged by opposing forces near the city of Tripoli, a PLO headquarters at the time. Only through the intervention of the United Nations were he and some of his supporters allowed to extricate themselves from the Syrian-supported militia seeking his demise. He subsequently moved his base to Tunisia, but following a deadly accurate Israeli bombing run he was asked to leave that residence as well.

In addition, random acts of terror have filled part of the vacuum that followed the defeat of the PLO in Lebanon. Particularly in Israel and on the West Bank, bands of youths, frustrated at the weakness of even its most radical leaders, have attacked civilians, bombed buses and shopping centers, and generally attempted to make a terrorist statement of their own. It is an ever-escalating set of circumstances, often out of control of even its proudest benefactors.

III

Ahmed is typical of a dying breed of West Bank intellectuals who try to maintain a moderate position in the midst of the turmoil. He is a senior staff member on one of Jerusalem's independent Arabic newspapers, and he spent several years in Jordanian prisons for his antiroyalist views. I meet with him as part of a small group of American Jewish journalists and academics.

He is short and round, in a white shirt and dark slacks. Even though it is pleasant in this shady garden outside Bethlehem, the summer heat has taken its toll on him. Ahmed loosens his collar and rolls up his sleeves as the perspiration drips from his face.

At all sides there are lean and swarthy young men whom he intro-duces as his sons and their friends. Ostensibly they are interested in hearing the comments and the tone of the discussion. But it is obvious that these are his bodyguards. This fellow understands the realities of life in these parts.

It is also obvious that Ahmed is polished and thoughtful. He under-stands the Western audience, what engages it and what impresses it. He has spent several months in residence at a major U.S. university and has met with similar groups in Israel. His facility with English is keen, and he is in every way master of the circumstances.

His opening statement is disarming. "What we need here," Ahmed begins, a soft smile creeping across his face, "is peaceful cooperation between Arabs and Jews to make this land a paradise. For us to fight each other is nonsense. We gain nothing by guns. But there will be no peace without a settlement with the Palestinians. Destroying the PLO will not bring peace."

Then his plea turns into an emotional, humanistic appeal. "We, the simple people of Palestine, want peace with Israel. We want our chil-dren to go with Israeli children to gardens and playgrounds. We want our money to build homes and industry. We want no war. The Pales-tinians are the Jews of the second half of the twentieth century. Let us work together to build a United States of the Middle East."

I look at the faces around me. Clearly, Ahmed has struck a respon-sive chord. It is novel for a Palestinian, any Palestinian, to call openly for cooperation and peace with Israel. The reference to children at play could hardly miss. The allusion to Palestinians as simple people seek-ing a homeland in the image of the Jew is unfair, but the point has taken hold. The choice of the phrase "a United States of the Middle East" conjures a free and peace-loving federation based on mutual respect and pluralistic democracy. I am impressed with Ahmed not for his courage so much as for his oratory.

"But why talk of Palestinian independence only after the land was taken by Israel? Couldn't there have been an independent or an auton-omous state created during nineteen years of Jordanian rule?" The question is posed flatly by a young writer from Detroit. It is his first foreign assignment and he scribbles notes anxiously as Ahmed re-flects.

He is not fazed by the parry. Instead, he answers with surprising candor. "Under Israel we have freedom, which is more than the rest of the Arab world has, I'm ashamed to tell you.'' There are knowing smiles all around. "When we have a state,'' he goes on, tipping his hand, but ever so slightly, "it will be a democracy, like Israel. Jordan is a medieval state, and Hussein is a small dictator backed by the United States.'' He speaks with all the bitterness and cynicism of one who has felt the brutality of Jordanian justice firsthand.

But Ahmed has made it clear that despite his moderate tone, the agenda still includes an independent Palestinian state, something most Israelis reject. The point has caught the group's attention. Yet he goes on, trying to build a credit balance for the more difficult debate yet to come.

"Why has the Palestinian movement grown under Israeli jurisdiction?'' he asks rhetorically. "Because we know that under Israel we will not be put in jail for our beliefs.'' He fairly spits the words on the table before him. "Most Arab ministers are thieves and bandits supported by the United States. The way to stop Communism in this part of the world,'' he says, irony dripping from every phrase, "is not to back corrupt regimes but to back the people.''

I engage Ahmed directly. Though not intentional on my part, the remainder of our meeting becomes a dialogue between the two of us. He appears to enjoy the repartee, though it embarrasses me to be thrust into this role. "Just who is Ahmed,'' I ask, "and what does he want? What is your vision for this part of the world?'' I don't mean it as a challenge, but he takes it that way, and apparently so do the others.

He smiles. "There is room for two nations on this land,'' he begins slowly, deliberately. "Let there be a State of Israel and an independent Palestinian state on the West Bank and Gaza. The two can live side by side.'' He pauses, as if to let the words sink in. The room is dead silent.

"The solution I seek would allow the new Palestinian state to join in some confederation with Jordan, but independence is a must.'' He neither trusts nor respects the Jordanians. "There can be two Jerusalems, jointly administered. Each sector would be the capital of one state and the entire unit capital of the new federation.'' His words echo the Jordanian option that the Labor Alignment has discussed publically for years. But with one difference. Ahmed wants a Palestinian state.

"You ask who am I and what is my vision,'' he goes on in the same rhetorical style. He is warming to the task and obviously enjoying himself. "I will tell you. I am a human being, not merely a branch cut from a tree and tossed from one corner to another. I don't want to challenge Israel in war. I want to challenge them in building schools. And," he concludes, a sly grin gradually filling his round face, "I am not ashamed to say that we will learn from the Israelis."

He is a skillful speaker. But I return to the front. What of the Israeli settlements on the territories? Will there be room for Jews in this new state he proposes? And what of the PLO? Speaking of peace and co-operation is fine, but the major Palestinian political units are bent on the "elimination of Zionism in Palestine." I think that I've scored points but Ahmed has been waiting for this. His answer is sincere, if a bit unrealistic.

"The PLO must change its covenant," he says matter-of-factly. "There must be mutual recognition, and this will only happen if the United States wants it to be. All Palestinian organizations, including the PLO, must renounce terrorism and violence, recognizing Israel's right to exist in peace and security. They should become political organizations that would compete for seats in a freely elected parliament. Leaders could then negotiate with Israel on the new federation that I see: the United States of the Middle East," he says again for emphasis.

"As far as Jewish settlements go," he says quietly, almost sadly, "they will have to be dismantled. Perhaps as we mature, it will be possible for us to live under the same roof. This early in our new relationship, I'm afraid there just won't be room for them." He is honest, frank, and naive.

But then, quickly, he shifts gears. His few words about the settlements interrupted him from the main stream of his thought. There is still something important that he wants to say by way of conclusion. It is a point that most people would not expect.

"Many of you are surprised to hear moderate words from a Palestinian," he begins. "The world has painted us as terrorists and radicals, mainly in the image of the PLO. But I must say, one of the reasons that the voice of moderation is not heard clearly among my people is Israel's refusal to allow political organization on the West Bank. Only well-financed, clandestine terrorist groups, like the PLO, have existed."

Ahmed pauses. He looks out into space, almost as if he is receiving otherworldly inspiration. Then his concentration returns. "Sometimes it seems like Israel would prefer to discourage moderates so that they won't have to deal with anyone but militants. The Israelis claim that they are looking for people of peace to negotiate, but it's easier to confront people of war. Why else do they prevent us from organizing?''

Our interview has ended. Ahmed walks from his table, past one of his ''sons'' who is holding the door for him. I smile as I watch them climb into their Mercedes. In a few seconds our meeting is little more than a cloud of white dust in the hot summer afternoon.

IV

Understanding, even empathizing with the position of West Bank Arabs is not generally the stock-in-trade of one who considers himself a loyal Zionist, especially in the Diaspora. Yet the issue really cuts right to the heart of Zionism as a Jewish national philosophy. It is part of a tension within the ideology that has dropped to the background in order to accommodate more pressing and practical matters, such as survival. But it can never disappear.

Zionism resulted from several strains of thought. Some partisans came to the commitment out of religious values, while others were avowed secularists. Some sought an alternative to the squalor and oppression of the countries of their birth, while others dreamed of social experimentation in a new society. But in all this, little was said about one fact that is central today.

The land that they came to already had inhabitants. It was not ''a land without people for a people without a land,'' as they imagined. Whether the land was bought outright or leased from an absentee pasha in Turkey or Syria mattered little to local Arab villagers. A deed or bill of sale was just some piece of paper. Possession counted. The Jewish passion for land purchase and legal niceties tended to create animosity, not the acceptance that it sought.

When early Zionists of whatever stripe considered the Arabs of Palestine at all, they usually came to one of three conclusions. Some argued that their presence was simply illegitimate and invalid. God had bequested the land to the children of Israel; it was part of his divine plan. These interlopers were there only as a result of various conquests over the years. It was a part of history to be erased by the return of the Jews to the land. Local peasants could either learn to live with their new overlords or get out. It really didn't make much difference.

Others who were more practical held that the Arabs of Palestine could be important political allies for early Jewish settlers. Each group had been promised a national homeland by the British. Each had an interest in promoting their claim with all possible dispatch. Jews lacked numbers and Arabs lacked social and political sophistication, but a union of the two communities would be irresistable.

Finally, there were those who viewed the presence of an Arab population in Palestine as momentous. They hoped to build an ethical civilization there, based on Jewish values and culture. Helping the peasants improve the quality of their lives, educating and working with them side by side, would be the most glorious accomplishment for Zionism. Not simply another conquest, it would be a grand partnership, a basic element of the just society to be built.

In retrospect, it all appears shortsighted and naive. Actually, many of these early Jewish settlers, and those who led or inspired them, probably didn't take these positions too seriously. For the most part, they just didn't think much about the Arabs of Palestine at all. They ignored them, hoping that they would somehow disappear. They were irrelevant to the Zionist cause; their presence was moot. At best, they were an unpleasant diversion from the task at hand.

The contemporary result of all this is a dichotomy between what Prof. Shlomo Avineri of the Hebrew University has called the "territorial" and "sociological" schools of modern Zionist thought. The first puts emphasis on the land and the crucial need to retain control of it, over and above questions of security and safety. For them, peace will only result from strong and secure boundaries properly armed. In any event, in this formulation, the land has a dynamic of its own, and matters of military strategy per se are really of secondary import.

The second position is more concerned with the quality of the Jewish state than its size or borders. As they see it, the Zionist dream was a state based on values and ethics. The Jewish homeland, they argue, must be more than just another country on the face of the map. Security will follow peace, they claim, and not the other way round.

Of course the differences are really of degree and emphasis rather than of kind. Territorialists are concerned with Jewish values and principles that, they assert, inform their position regarding the land of

Israel. By the same token, proponents of the sociological school also love the land and display their loyalty by going to the front in its defense. It is precisely this love for the land that informs their desire to create a more just society within its borders, they argue.

Out of this last set of concerns, moral judgments emerge regarding the inevitable evil that comes from being an occupier. No matter how benign the occupation, no matter how the vanquished population gains from its patronage, the result too often leads to brutality. This is as damaging to the perpetrator as to his victim. This is not what Zionism intended, they argue.

Listen to Eli, a student at Tel Aviv University: "It's not necessary to go into all the gory details. The papers are filled with the bloodshed and the beatings. Arab children dispersed by force; teenagers shot by Israeli soldiers; settlers rampaging through Arab towns, ruining stores and shops and then demanding an apology for some imagined injury to their pride. And that's not the worst of it."

He has hit a nerve. A nation justly proud of its democratic and humanitarian institutions now finds itself accused of abuses against a captive population. Much of the violence reported is the result of confrontations between Jewish settlers and local Arabs, with vigilantism on both sides. It's difficult to assign blame in such cases; there are usually excesses on both sides. It's even more complicated when settlers are also reservists in the Israeli army.

The Israeli military has always been a hotly political affair. When there is an incident, it's a sure bet that among those charged with keeping the peace are uniformed Israelis who live on the territories themselves or sympathize with those who do. This impinges on military discipline and creates poor morale among their bunkmates who believe otherwise.

The accusation that Israel is oppressing others, denying them legal or political expression, is an ugly rub for many of its people. How can we do to others what was done to us for centuries? they ask. Don't we know better? Don't we understand? "Maybe you can kill a person and break up a rally," Eli concludes, "but you can't kill an idea and break up a movement."

Added to this is the matter of numbers. There are about 750,000 Arabs living on the West Bank, excluding Jerusalem and there are an additional half million on the Gaza Strip. If Israel were to annex these territories, it would inherit a large and hostile mass, presumably eligible for all the rights and benefits of citizenship. They would immediately constitute roughly 40 percent of Israel's population.

As protagonists are quick to recall, the Arab birthrate is generally higher than the Jewish one. In a generation or less, these new fellow countrymen would outnumber their former overlords. They wouldn't have to call for the creation of an independent Palestinian state by means of international violence and terror. They could simply vote one into existence and compromise the Jewish complexion of Israel itself. The thought is chilling.

The alternative is equally chilling. Having incorporated the territories, Israel could create a two-tiered system of citizenship. Jews and Arabs within the 1967 borders, for example, would continue to enjoy all the rights and privileges they have now. But the political prerogatives of the newcomers would have to be severely restricted. To allow them to vote, assemble, or have access to the media would invite disaster.

Turning Israel into what Rhodesia was, or what South Africa and Northern Ireland are today, is morally unacceptable to many Israelis. So is the idea of expelling Arab residents on a mass scale, no matter how gently or benevolently. But there is a far more crucial dimension. This kind of official action would undermine Israel's democracy and wreak civil strife. It could rock the society to its very foundations and turn Israel into an armed camp.

V

Prophecy is difficult, an old proverb has it, especially when it is about the future. But the most disturbing projection regarding Arab life on the West Bank and its relationship to one or another Israeli government is that ten years down the road nothing will have changed. No representative West Bank leadership will emerge to open negotiations with an amenable Israeli cabinet, nor will credible Arab leaders or terrorist strongmen join the peace process.

Instead, the bloodletting that continues in Lebanon will serve as a convenient excuse for delay. While Christians, Sunnis, Shiites, Druze, and just about everyone else vent their ancient animosities in all directions, all other considerations must be put on hold. Perhaps the Palestinian issue is much less central to the Middle East conflict than anyone imagines. Even if it were solved, the Lebanese would war as Iran and Iraq plod toward their seventh year of battle and both Syria and Libya covetously eye the territory of their neighbors.

This goes far toward explaining why the simplest part of the whole affair, the refugee problem, has yet to be resolved. Given the enormous wealth available to the Arab world and the technology at the disposal of the United Nations, there is no reason that hundreds of thousands of Palestinians should still live in refugee camps on the territories, in Jordan, and in southern Lebanon.

There are no financial or logistical reasons, that is, but there are important political reasons. Bulldozing the camps and resettling their residents would allow the refugees to become assimilated into their host communities. It would mean that they could pursue their own interests and try to raise families in something approaching normalcy. That is what neither the host countries nor Palestinian militants would like to see happen.

For were it to occur, these refugees would lose their radical fighting edge. They might abandon their ideological and dogmatic hatreds and move headlong into the conservative middle class, pursuing such mundane concerns as making a living and saving for college. Militants would lose their constituency as a result, and the royal house of Jordan, for example, would inherit a threatening bloc of educated and demanding citizens.

In fact, this is precisely what happened to those Palestinians who came to southern Lebanon in the late 1940s and early 1950s. Many accepted Lebanese citizenship, opened businesses, and raised families. For over twenty years they accommodated themselves to the hospitable environment that Lebanon offered, and by the early 1970s they occupied a position of singular success among their brethren.

But in 1970, King Hussein expelled the PLO from its base in Jordan in an operation that stalwarts still refer to as Black September. The organization's leadership moved its forces to southern Lebanon, building an empire based on brutality and unspeakable atrocity. Women and children were violated, whole sections of towns were razed, and terrorist training camps were established to welcome the political misfits of the world.

The result was the Lebanese civil war of 1975–76 that led Syria into Lebanese territory to prevent the PLO from simply overrunning the country. It was the prelude to the Israeli invasions of the late 1970s and early 1980s in which, ironically, Syria became the unwitting protector of the PLO. Ultimately, it led to the truncated entity that is Lebanon today.

Those Palestinians who had arrived in southern Lebanon a generation or so earlier suffered miserably. They were exploited and terrorized by the very people who claimed to represent their national interest, all because they dared to live peaceful and productive lives.

This is why it serves the purposes of Palestinian militants to continue having refugees and refugee camps. These are the breeding grounds for tomorrow's guerrilla martyrs, the schools for terror and hatred. Nor would King Hussein or any of his Arab League associates like to have the whole mess dumped into their political laps.

Finally, in a very real sense, there are features of Israeli life, both political and cultural, that play into the hands of militants and that encourage Arab radicalism on the territories and elsewhere. There is little effective separation between the Palestinians and the most extreme elements of the PLO, for example. Instead, a self-fulfilling prophecy tends to operate, one that suggests that only radicals genuinely speak for the people. The only way to deal with such militancy is with equal measures of force and resolution.

This fits neatly with a more general belief about Arabs, be they adversaries or fellow citizens. It is widely held that Israeli liberalism and moderation will be interpreted as weakness. The only language that Arabs understand is force, and signs of indecision will inevitably be exploited. This view is joined by a myopic understanding of traditional Arab life, where authority patterns tend to be personalized. Villages, clans, and tribes generally depend upon an individual leader or family to represent their best interests before any central administration. In the grand style of the political club house, patronage is distributed according to one's contacts, loyalty, and support.

By contrast, Israeli administration on the territories has attempted to approximate the image of political reform. There are instances of favoritism and personal influence, to be sure, but more common is the desire to treat all claims and demands among local Arabs equally, without regard to political ideology, commitment, or affiliation.

With the exception of elected figures who lend public support to militancy and extremism, radicals and moderates alike have had equal access to or distance from the seats of power. By and large, there have been no formal rewards for moderation or disincentives toward violence. In many ways, the PLO injected itself into a political vacuum.

By the same token, this may also be part of a grand Israeli scenario. Despite Shimon Peres's recent call for Arab leaders, indeed even Soviet leaders, to join in negotiation, the Israelis don't have to do much as long as no one accepts. They can loudly proclaim that they're waiting for a moderate Palestinian to come forward and just gear themselves for a confrontation with militants.

They won't need any contingency plans for dealing with militants. They can claim that everything is open to negotiation without having to make difficult choices. Perhaps they are hoping that no moderates will emerge. The point was reflected in the words of a keen observer, an Arab journalist from Nablus. "This is the Middle East, you know. With whom you have lunch is an important item, a means of power." The table is set, the hosts are ready—but they seem to be hoping that no one will come to dinner.

PART THREE

Zionism: Keeping the Promise Alive

8

American Zionism: Continuity and Change

I

There is a periodic disturbance that emerges in the minds of U.S. Jewish leaders regarding Israel and Zionism. The contemporary American Jew, they fear, has lost his sense of urgency about the Jewish stake in the Middle East. He has been overtaken by his own material needs and is more likely to be driven by them in forming his personal values and setting his communal agenda. Unlike the situation in times past, they charge, Israel is no longer a first priority in the social and political consciousness of the U.S. Jewish community.

In particular, they fear for the youth. A common theme in many refrains is the portrayal of young people as the forefront of this headlong move toward affluence and assimilation. Part of their newfound enlightenment is a tendency to question old commitments of every order, including those that link American Jews to Israel. Yuppies, we are told, just don't have time for such things.

The trepidation generally reaches its peak in October and early November, especially, though not exclusively, in those years when a U.S. president is to be elected. Israel must be reaffirmed as the first issue for Jewish voters of all persuasions. Candidates must be impressed

This chapter is an expanded and updated version of "American Zionism: Continuity and Change," originally published in *Tradition*, vol. 20, Summer 1982.

with the idea that there is no other way to attract Jewish support, whether electoral, financial, or otherwise.

To match these objectives, a parallel campaign must be undertaken to raise the consciousness (a media term that smacks of surgical jargon) of both those standing for election and those standing in line to elect. There must be a massive effort to galvanize candidates and voters alike and to ward off the most dangerous of all enemies, apathy. Consequently, during each election pious statements abound regarding the need to reclaim Zionist commitment among our youth. Recriminations are leveled over the lack of enthusiasm displayed by one or another group. Perhaps more than anything else, there is much worrying.

On the face of it, however, it appears that a good deal of this angst is unnecessary, or at least misplaced. To the extent that we may identify Zionism with support for Israel—and there will be some who object to this identification—the U.S. Jewish community has been "Zionized."

The battles of the past—fears of dual loyalty, the Pittsburgh Platform, and the American Council for Judaism—have not so much been won as made irrelevant. They remain primarily as historical curiosities, to be dusted off every now and again for polemic and ideological purposes. Zionist organizations tend to have long memories.

In sum, it may be that support for Israel among most Jews in the United States is far more an emotional than an intellectual enterprise. At the very least, it appears to have elicited a response in the vast majority of its constituents. There are data to support the position. For example, a recent survey of U.S. Jewish attitudes toward Israel and Zionism, commissioned by the American Jewish Committee, made the point plainly.* Most essentially, the research indicated that U.S. Jews overwhelmingly support Israel by every standard definition of the term. Over 90 percent said that they paid special attention to media reports about Israel, and a similar proportion declared themselves "pro-Israel" or "very pro-Israel." In addition, about three-quarters said that caring about Israel was a very important part of their Jewish identity and that they frequently talked about Israel with friends and relatives.

Of course, the fact that U.S. Jews declare their support for Israel is

---

*Steven M. Cohen, *Attitudes of American Jews Toward Israel and Israelis* (New York: American Jewish Committee, 1983).

hardly a revelation. More to the point, the study also suggested that they were very much at ease with that declaration. They saw no trouble with that support as it related to their identifications as Americans. Thus over 90 percent responded that support for Israel was in the best interests of the United States and that they felt no discomfort about it. In addition, some three-quarters noted that they saw no conflict between their "devotion to Israel" and their loyalties to the United States. About the same number indicated that Jews should not vote for candidates who were unfriendly to Israel.

II

Before proceeding, however, three points need to be made in regard to these findings: two explanatory and the other plainly editorial. First, in many ways, support for Israel among U.S. Jews is a reactive phenomenon, that is, their interest in the Middle East relates profoundly to what they perceive around them. They do not yet feel secure in the United States. For many, Israel is their most efficacious conduit for ethnic identity. Once again, a brief foray into some recent statistical data is enlightening.

A recent study, carried out under the auspices of the American Jewish Committee, was intended to evaluate the presence of anti-Semitism in America.* As a secondary objective, however, the study compared gentile attitudes with those ascribed to them by U.S. Jews. The differences are dramatic, indeed little short of startling. Overall they indicate a low level of anti-Semitic feeling within the U.S. population generally, contrasted with a clear sense of insecurity and suspicion among Jews regarding what their gentile neighbors believe.

To choose a few brief examples, a sample of non-Jews were asked whether they felt that Jews had too much power in the U.S. business establishment. Some 32 percent answered in the affirmative. When Jews were asked what they thought their gentile neighbors would say, 76 percent declared that gentiles believed that Jews had too much power in business.

Similarly, only 16 percent of gentile respondents agreed that "Jews try to push themselves where they are not wanted." Among Jews in

*Based on data presented in Daniel Yankelovich, "Summary Report," *Anti-Semitism in the United States* (New York: American Jewish Committee, 1981).

the sample, 55 percent said that gentiles would affirm that belief. Finally, 77 percent of Jewish respondents felt that gentiles would be bothered that "Jews have more money than most people." By contrast, only 13 percent of non-Jews answered that question in the affirmative.

This discomfort is somewhat paradoxically joined by a growing disaffection from Jewish life, another factor in Israel's primacy for so many U.S. Jews. In particular, it is reflected in the substantial numbers who have chosen to disassociate themselves from Judaism as an organized faith.

Thus a variety of national surveys of U.S. Jews have suggested that as many as 40 percent have no synagogue affiliation whatsoever. Whatever else may contribute to their ethnic identity, U.S. Jewish religious institutions have been less than a rousing success.

The point weighs heavily on our discussion. Apparently, a large proportion of America's Jews are uncomfortable and insecure in their environs. They reflect a deep but somewhat unjustified suspicion of the beliefs and the motivations of their non-Jewish neighbors. For them, Israel has become vitally important not as a living alternative but more so as a refuge, a final port in the storms of humanity, should the unthinkable occur once more.

By the same token, if a substantial minority of U.S. Jews find little comfort in their synagogues and temples, then Israel becomes for them the bulk (perhaps the sum) of their Jewish identity. "Being Jewish" means caring about news reports from the Middle East, purchasing an Israel bond, or planting a tree with the Jewish National Fund. Once again, the support and affiliation is reactive, negative at best.

Secondly, and more practically, the importance of Israel in the minds of even marginally affiliated U.S. Jews is something of a self-fulfilling prophecy. Jewish organizations, for example, have become firm believers in the Zionist cause, and this includes many community-based organizations that tended to eschew such public positions in the past. In response to the fears and trepidations noted earlier, they mount major efforts to lobby for an ever-increasing helping of psychic, political, and fiscal Zionism from among their members. They are similarly driven in their relations with the media, with leaders of other ethnic and religious communities, and with public officials.

In return, candidates for election or public officials seeking to curry favor with Jewish constituents will take their cues from Jewish organizational leaders. Their prime contacts with the community are lodged within these agencies, and they accept this formula for Jewish support as a given: if you want to reach Jewish voters, you have to be "right on Israel." Consequently, they build support for Israel into their platforms and position papers and feed it back to the community, in roughly the same form that it was extended to them. The media covers these attempts and then evaluates one or another candidate in this context. It's as if that's all there is!

This is not to suggest that Israel's needs are not a priority to the rank-in-file of these organizations or that the entire enterprise is purely self-serving. It is rather to suggest that what has been true before becomes truer still; what may have been vague and mistlike now becomes material and real.

A basic tendency is now reinforced by powerful elements of the communal and electoral process mobilized in formidable symbiosis. Even Jewish voters who might stray to other issues are engaged first in terms of their Zionism by candidates, media, and organizations both inside and outside the community. The sum of it points to their positions and their track records as they attempt to outdo each other in support for Israel.

Finally, Zionism—for better or for worse, but primarily for convenience—has been generally identified here with support for Israel. But Zionist commitment should emphatically not be mistaken for the extent to which one is willing to accept a maximalist position in the Israel-Arab conflict. Demanding immediate settlement or annexation of the West Bank/Judea and Samaria, for example, is not necessarily "good Zionism." Neither is one "soft on Zionism" if one believes a reconciliatory strategy to be more wise, even if it includes territorial concessions.

The key is the commitment to Israel's needs and its centrality in reaching these conclusions. Parenthetically, shouting these conclusions at the Israeli government from the op-ed pages of the New York Times is not so much bad Zionism as it is bad sense.

In the same vein, it is erroneous and unfortunate that the degree of Zionist commitment has rapidly become linked to religious belief and ritual practice. In some strange and confusing calculus, rabbis are expected to be more Zionist than lay people. Similarly, those who are traditionally observant are assumed to be more militant in their defense of Israel's welfare than those who eat ham.

The point was epitomized at a recent meeting of a major Jewish organization attempting to coordinate the pro-Israel efforts of its constituent units. One member was in the midst of an impassioned tirade in support of West Bank settlement as a basis for Israel's security. As he went on in the most vehement fashion, one gray-haired executive leaned over to his neighbor. The two whispered for a brief while. Finally, their conversation ended sotto voce. "What do you expect?" said the first. "He's Orthodox!"

No matter the contemporary imagery; let the record stand clear. Israel's founding and its survival have never been purely a function of religious thought or traditional observance. To the contrary, Zionist leadership—ideological, political, and military—has generally been spawned from the secular element of the Jewish community. Rabbis and pietists have been rather slow to join the parade, and when they have, it has been haltingly and with more than a few misgivings. Some still haven't joined.

In that regard, there has been a noteworthy loss to Zionism and Israel's well-being both in the United States and in the Holy Land. Once energetic and proud, many secular, socialist, and revisionist Zionist organizations have become mere shells. Their youth wings sorely need revitalization. Their presidia beg for a transfusion of fresh blood.

For our purposes it must be reemphasized that support for Israel should not be related to synagogue attendance, nor does it depend on the brand of meat one places on his table. It is a mitzvah, a precept of its own, and one that can be fulfilled equally by the religious, the secular, or the agnostic.

III

Having said all this, there is still cause for Zionist concern. But it is a concern different from that which has generally been expressed. Before we go about wringing our hands or undertaking a media blitz, it is imperative that we understand just what seems to have taken place.

It does not appear that the quantity of Jewish support for Israel has waned in the general population. However, there do seem to be important though subtle qualitative changes that demand closer scrutiny. Truly, these qualitative changes, while not exclusive to the young, may be more pronounced among them.

First is an obvious fact of simple demography whose impact on

Zionist commitment seems to have eluded even the sharpest of ideologues. An entire generation has emerged in the past forty years that simply cannot be expected to respond to the Zionist call in the same reflexive fashion as their parents often do, nor ought we expect them to.

This is a generation for whom Israel is not so much a cause as a given. It is a generation that has never known a world without a Jewish state, a generation for whom the endless debates over the wisdom and the nature of Jewish statehood—as well as the realities of gunrunning and arms smuggling—are mere curiosities of history. All this assumes that they are aware of these things at all!

It is also a generation that did not experience the Holocaust. Despite their contemporary fascination with the horror, its members cannot recall a world in which Jews had no place to go, no friendly port, no city of refuge. In facing that fact today, some exhibit a morbid sensationalism thirsting for testaments and firsthand reports of the horror, in the name of bearing witness. Others manage to elicit a vicarious shock in an increasingly jaded world. They use it to cement their newfound militancy as they loudly proclaim ''never again.'' Still others approach it all with antiseptic scholarship, analyzing and detailing to distraction while deriving no more emotional punch than any history text can offer.

The sum of it all is quite direct, among those born after World War II—a group defined as ''youth'' only in the loosest terms. For them, Israel is less the fulfillment of a messianic dream whose seeds emerge from centuries of religious and national longing than it is a simple fact of international life.

Their commitment to Israel is pervasive and strong, to be sure. Still, it lacks much of the passion and emotional thrust that it continues to pack for their elders. It is unreasonable to expect that they will develop a feverish reaction to the specifics of a boundary dispute or the wisdom of an arms sale. In fact, these issues may be little more than tiresome.

Consequently, it makes little sense approaching this audience with traditional Zionist rhetoric. Appeals to the age-old dream of a people or the need for a place of refuge will likely miss their mark. Suggesting that Israel is the only legitimate home for a Jew may be well intentioned and even justifiable, but it will offend far more than it will attract.

Similarly, portraying Israel in purely subordinate and philanthropic terms may raise funds, but it may have a demoralizing (and perhaps counterproductive) effect as well. The life or death of the State of Israel does not hinge on every question of U.S. Middle East policy, nor is every fund-raising campaign the one upon which Jewish survival depends. History and experience defy such gimmickry.

Unfortunately, far too many Jewish communal workers and development professionals are evaluated on the basis of their ability to turn such phrases and the dollars or numbers that are generally thought to be linked to them. For them, there is a stake in creating an air of consistent hysteria, sometimes only marginally related to reality. The thought was brought home in the words of one leading administrator of a Zionist fund-raising agency. He offered his analysis of fiscal prospects to a group of field representatives for the year following the Israeli Lebanon campaign. "Things will be tough," he concluded, a pained expression slowly covering his face. "Unfortunately, there's no war on this year."

Attracting this segment of the Jewish public will require greater candor and less hysteria, though not necessarily less emotion. A shift in the way Israel is portrayed to its friends seems in order. It must not be seen as a ward of the United States and a pitiable recipient of charity from Jewish protectors abroad. Instead, it must be characterized more in the form of a junior partner with the United States in its confrontations with adversaries internationally. The Reagan administration has opened the door by identifying the Soviet Union as the consummate threat to U.S. interests in the Middle East and elsewhere. To the extent that Arab radicalism serves as the Soviet Union's client, Israel stands as the major bulwark against Soviet expansion in this strategic area.

Further, even compared with those Arab powers that have been identified as moderate or friendly to U.S. interests, Israel remains the most reliable ally. It is the single polity in the Middle East whose government can tolerate a transfer of power and a change in leadership. It has withstood political and economic hardship and has never waivered from support of U.S. policy in international bodies. The latter virtue, in particular, is something that no Arab nation—indeed that few others anywhere in the world—can claim.

In addition, though not obviously involved in the confrontation, oil-rich sheikhdoms of the Persian Gulf have been bankrolling radicalism and terror in the Middle East and elsewhere for decades. No one need document the fact that Americans have increasingly been the targets of such terror thousands of miles from the ostensible theater of battle.

These are points worth making as the descriptions of "moderate and friendly" are bestowed by the U.S. State Department. They are also important though not exclusive appeals for less emotional and more secular Jewish audiences. They serve as the foundation for an approach to those whose dedication requires something more than tradition and hymn.

No matter how it may pain their elders, the issue carries still another implication. These younger Jews, particularly of the West, do not consider themselves displaced persons or protected minorities living at the pleasure of some noble. Instead, they proudly proclaim themselves citizens of their land of residence, with more than a little interest and commitment to its standing and welfare.

For the vast majority, aliyah, the call to Jewish settlement in Israel, is simply not an option. With rare exception they will continue living comfortably in the Diaspora and will encourage their children to do likewise. In their minds, Israel is less a homeland than a refuge of last resort.

Consequently, for Zionism to continue its rejection of the Diaspora flies in the face of reality. More importantly, it wins few friends. On the contrary, far too many of Israel's most loyal constituents in the West recognize that were it not for the constant support of Diaspora Jewish communities, Zionist prospects might well be bleak.

Jews throughout the world have accomplished much in the postwar era. In both secular and parochial terms, they have been extraordinarily successful. There is much that they will yet contribute to their host communities as well as to the welfare of the State of Israel. Insisting that aliyah be the sole legitimate purpose to their Zionist commitment is not so much wrong as it is counterproductive.

IV

If there has been a qualitative shift in the nature of Zionist support among many U.S. Jews, there has also been a matching change in the qualitative nature of its object: the State of Israel. Rightly or wrongly, American Jews no longer sense an urgency about Israel; they no longer feel that its very survival is threatened from without. A good measure of that feeling stems from their own encounters with Israel and with Israelis.

Instead, they perceive Israel's existence as largely assured. In fact, they see it as the major military power in the Middle East. The perception is closely related to Israeli military success matched by its promotion of that prowess in the public relations and media mills of the globe. With U.S. support, perhaps even without it, the apparent threat to Israel from without reaches nowhere near its jugular. Nothing succeeds like success.

More crucially, there are important domestic changes manifest in Israel that have contributed to shifts in U.S. Jewish support. These changes are not always happy ones. As among Jews in the United States, the issues facing Israel today are not nearly so clear and definitive as they once were, and the impact is felt on both sides of the ocean.

What began as an exciting social experiment, merging traditional beliefs with liberal lifestyles in the wake of the Holocaust, seems to have soured. The image of the Jewish phoenix, rising to life from its own ashes, for many has receded. Somehow, the excitement is gone. Instead, Israeli life, its popular culture, its speech, dress, and aspirations appear to the outsider as cheap imitations. Rather than a new Jewish expression, they are a pale shadow of the American original. A stroll down Dizengoff Road in Tel Aviv, for example, tends not to leave one with any particularly Jewish feelings.

Except in certain limited (and limiting) circles, the commitment to a peculiarly Jewish state is nearly gone. The very lack of commitment that is bemoaned among U.S. Jews is hardly more evident among most Israelis, except, perhaps, those affiliated with the tourist industry or the immigration agencies.

Instead, Zionist thinking is viewed as rather quaint in Israel. Perhaps it is appropriate to foreign fund-raising efforts or diplomatic conferences, but it has little to do with the realities and aspirations of everyday life.

Indeed, within Israel, the debate over its direction and the quality of its life is rampant and well publicized. It is a debate that informs many of the shifts in sentiment perceived abroad. From economics to religion, from ethnic accommodation to national security, there appears to be only vague consensus on the general and very little on the specific. Not too many years ago many of these rifts were papered over in the name of the great overriding commitment. "Ayn Brera," the Israeli would shrug. "Sure we'd like to confront all these issues, but for now we have no choice. Parochial needs must be sacrificed for the demands of sheer survival."

As Israel has become more of an established power than a fledgling experiment, however, as the issue of survival has lost its overarching hold, so too has its invocation lost its effectiveness in matters of domestic need. One can hardly blame a U.S. Jew (or non-Jew, for that matter) if now and again some cynicism betrays his general support for Israeli policy. Nor should he be expected to reflexively assume a maximalist position on every matter of military strategy or international diplomacy. After all, most Israelis refuse to. The results of Israel's last two national elections—the one a "dead heat," the other followed by confusion and disarray—underscore the point.

Of course, Israelis have been confirming this change in their Zionist/national commitment through a different election: one in which they have been voting with their feet. Depending on whose numbers are accepted, somewhere between 250,000 and 400,000 Israelis have emigrated to the United States since 1948. Their motivations and lifestyles will be discussed elsewhere, but their presence must be noted here.

It is a presence that has left its mark on U.S. Jews. Israelis arriving on these shores have not always made a favorable impression upon their coreligionists, possibly because Americans have unrealistic expectations of them. The clash leaves both sides the worse for it. For example, their motivations for leaving Israel are generally couched in economic terms: they are here *lehistader*, to set themselves up. In this they are much like immigrants from other countries or the grandparents of contemporary U.S. Jews.

Notwithstanding, their rush to taste all that this country has to offer frequently creates for them an image of crass and unthinking materialism, so, too, their willingness to exert themselves at jobs that they would have considered beneath them in Israel. It is certainly not the stuff of which *halutzim*, Jewish pioneers, are made. Similarly, their candid lack of religious values is a disappointment, especially to those who have come to erroneously link Zionist spirit with some brand of religious orthodoxy. Finally, their apparent willingness to assimilate themselves and their children into the American middle class is a cruel rejection of the very foundations of Zionism.

Perhaps it is improper for one who lives in the magnificent glass mansion that is the United States to throw ideological stones, but if we note a qualitative change in contemporary Zionist spirit, it must be studied in Israel as well as in the United States. The changes in Israel (and among Israelis) have not been lost on U.S. Jews.

V

The qualitative changes in U.S. Zionism are also reflections of important quantitative changes that have taken place in the past generation. For example, demography has not been kind to U.S. Jews. Economically and socially based decisions to limit family size have not only decreased their numbers but have disproportionately arranged age distributions. In simple terms, Jews are a rapidly aging people, perhaps the oldest ethnic group in the United States. The social implications of this development and those that have contributed to it are discussed at length elsewhere in this book, but a word about their political impact is in order, especially as it relates to support for Israel among U.S. Jews.

As the community ages, its senior members, who have served in leadership positions over the years, are moving on. Having done their share, they will rightfully expect to be replaced by enthusiastic newcomers. A younger leadership cadre should be in the process of development right now for that inevitable eventuality, but the pool of newcomers is becoming increasingly thin. Many lack the zeal. Others lack the training and background. By dint of demography alone, still others are simply not there. Pity the successor generation.

The aging trend is reinforced by a parallel development: outward mobility. In the first case, many retirees have chosen to leave the big cities of their youth and middle age in return for the sun and relaxation of the South and Southwest. Along Miami's Collins Avenue, signs prohibiting trespassing—written in English, Spanish, and Yiddish— reflect this well-known development.

In addition to this exodus of the elderly, there has been a parallel stream of younger Jewish families following the national move to the sun. Some have been drawn by the decision of large corporations to quit the Northeast and relocate where labor costs and taxes are lower. Others have been genuinely lured by the more relaxed lifestyle and the quality of housing and public services. Whatever the motives, the re-

sult has been the establishment of small Jewish enclaves in rather unlikely places. As a reflection, Jewish candidates have been elected in
Kansas, Arizona, and other localities not previously known as *Yidisher
gegent.* Only in America!

The development is not without at least two political costs, and,
after all, it is through Jewish political clout that support for Israel is
most effectively expressed. One is also the result of demography, while
the other is related to a quirk in the U.S. electoral system.

The growing trend toward intermarriage among America's Jews has
been discussed earlier. Suffice it to say here that while national rates
of Jewish intermarriage are increasing, they are still higher in small-
town America with its minuscule Jewish populations. In some cases,
the substantial majority of Jews who marry there, marry non-Jews.

Attachment to Israel is one element—perhaps the premier element—
in a constellation of Jewish values. Assimilation, intermarriage, secularism, and other attending social phenomena must have an inevitably
deleterious effect upon active communal and Zionist involvement. The
loss of young Jewish couples, and their children drives our median
age still higher and gnaws yet further at our bank of potential leaders.
The rush to the sun that we are experiencing only fans and encourages
that development.

In addition, even for those who retain their Jewish commitments in
the same magnitude as before, the movement of Jewish families to
smaller communities in nonindustrial states has a negative impact upon
the aggregate of Jewish political influence. This is due to a subtle
peculiarity in the U.S. electoral system that is rather complex. National elections here are based not on a direct vote but upon a complicated (some suggest antiquated) means for choosing a president known
as the electoral college. For some, this appears to be merely a rubber
stamp that simply confirms what the general election has already decided, but that's not quite true.

As presently constituted, the system favors large, urban, and industrial states by assigning them substantial blocs of electoral votes, win-
ner take all. Consequently, Jews and other minorities, housed for generations in or near these urban centers, have had a disproportionate
influence on national elections. After all, a few thousand votes could
put a state in the candidate's column.

Because these pivotal groups were favored by geography, presidential candidates have been forced to pay closer attention to their needs

and demands. However, the dissipation of such strategic concentrations, whether by virtue of mature or youthful mobility, can only weaken Jewish political strength nationally. In simple terms, moving to the sun may mean moving away from traditional political influence.

There is a parallel development that underlines these thoughts. One of American Jewry's great political strengths has been its propensity toward the vote. Though Jews have always represented a small minority, even in those areas where they were heavily concentrated, they could always bring in the vote. They tended to turn out at the polls in greater proportion than their numbers in the population might suggest, and that's still true.

Yet, almost as if to reflect the broader tendency of the next generation to gradually divest itself of its links with the past, younger Jews tend to vote with less regularity than do their elders. As a result, even within their adopted communities in parts of the country new to Jewish residence, they may have less political influence than they did a generation ago.

Any reevaluation of Zionist commitment must therefore be linked to a continued appreciation of this fundamental form of political activism. Deeds must follow words. You can't be taken seriously if your people don't show up. Here, too, U.S. Jews seem to be changing.

VI

Finally, the nature of U.S. Zionist commitment has been affected by secular political changes in the United States. The point has been explored at length in chapter 4. The predominant values of U.S. political leadership of the 1980s appear to be conservative, at least in the short run. It behooves Zionist leaders, therefore, to hone their approaches toward this constituency as an avenue for increased cooperation and alliance between the United States and Israel. With the support and encouragement of Israel's resurgent right, this is precisely what they have been doing. They must bear in mind, however, that neither theological, cultural, nor political sense is observed by an alliance between the Zionist community and the evangelical/conservative coalition.

There is no better way to conclude this essay than to return it to its beginning. Despite much well-publicized angst, the U.S. Jewish community is staunchly behind Israel and its needs. Support for Israel remains a priority, and so it will continue to be for the foreseeable future. But America's Jews have undergone important qualitative changes in the last generation. Some are significant in their own right and affect Zionism only peripherally. Others directly confront Zionist ideology and affect the strength of sympathy with Israel.

In either instance, it behooves leaders both here and in Israel to reconsider the symbiotic relationship that exists between these two large and powerful Jewish communities, a process that should be ongoing in any event. The following suggestions serve to summarize what has been said here:

- New, less emotional appeals should be directed toward a generation of Jews for whom Israel is a reality and not necessarily the fulfillment of a messianic dream.
- Zionist leaders should reconsider their rejection of the Diaspora and their traditional emphasis on aliyah, at least for rhetorical purposes, especially in their relations with Western Jews.
- If the alleged Zionist malaise in the United States is cause for much anxiety and concern, it should be seen as related to a similar and reciprocal development in Israel itself.
- The effect of demographic changes in the U.S. Jewish community upon the structure and the quality of U.S. Zionism should be taken into account.
- Finally, the newly forged alliances between Israeli and Zionist leaders and the conservative right in the United States should be carefully considered, particularly in regard to evangelical Christians. In fact, the alliance may be more trouble than it is worth.

Truly, there have been changes in the nature of U.S. Zionist support, but the changes will not be accommodated by hand-wringing and recrimination. Nor are they susceptible to the common bureaucratic rush to divest one's organization from responsibility and hide behind well-worn rhetoric and thunder.

Too often we are overtaken by something similar to the recent thinking of a popular cartoon character. "I know that I could easily light a candle," he suggests, in light that renders him barely visible to the reader. "But frankly, I find cursing the darkness far more emotionally rewarding."

9

Yordim: Zionism in Reverse

I

"Sami, *od kos kaffee*—another cup of Turkish coffee please." The small restaurant is like dozens found throughout Israel. The young men are lean, dark, and swarthy. One or two wear *kippot*, knitted skull caps. Most do not.

There are two girls watching a game of *shesh-besh*, backgammon. They, too, are olive skinned, in tight jeans and tangles of chains. The radio blares Israeli pop. Tonight it's Simon and Garfunkel in Hebrew. Dispersed throughout the room are couples in fours and eights doing what Israelis love best: talking the night away. Their speech is clipped and punctuated with loud laughter and occasional shouts of anger or emphasis.

The scene is not unlike hundreds in Tel Aviv, Jerusalem, or Haifa. Locals are out for an evening of relaxation and good fun. Yet it takes place in none of these cities. Instead it is in a small storefront on a side street in Brooklyn. The patrons are locals, a new breed of Israeli known as *yordim*. The term comes from the verb "to descend," and it refers to a talmudic belief that one who goes to the Holy Land ascends spiritually. Ergo, one who leaves, descends. Its implications,

This chapter is an expanded and updated version of "Yored is also a Noun," originally published in *Midstream*, February 1978.

though, are much more derogatory than some rabbinic reference might suggest. To be a *yored* is to be an expatriot: one part coward, one part deserter, and one part traitor.

While there has always been a stream of Israelis to the United States, the flow appears to have reached substantial proportions since the 1973 Yom Kippur War. It is officially estimated that there are about 150,000 yordim in the New York area, for example. Unofficial counts suggest twice that number. Much to the dismay of Israeli authorities, the flow does not appear to be ebbing. Israeli residential centers have developed in many cities throughout the country. They have made their presence felt in restaurants, in boutiques, and in medical centers, at beauty parlors and at universities.

The response of Israeli officialdom has been predictably harsh. Parliamentary debates over the issue have deteriorated into shouting matches. Yordim are called "nemushot" (weak) and "bogdim" (traitors). In a fit of pique, Defense Minister Yitzhak Rabin referred to these émigrés as "napolet shel mishud," loosely, the droppings of bugs. As one right-wing deputy put it: "The Diaspora is a disease, and we should have nothing to do with those who join it."

Yet the patrons of this little café are neither traitors nor cowards. They certainly have the stamp of Israel in their speech, mannerisms, and dress. What they appear to exhibit more than anything else is a sense of guilt.

"I am here for thirteen years, yet I still consider myself an Israeli," says Tommy, a shopkeeper. "Life here is cold and unfriendly; you can't enjoy yourself with Americans. People are closer and talk to strangers in Israel. Here no one wants to know you!"

Sami agrees. His family owns the restaurant. "I am here only about one year," he says in halting English. "I thought it would be good here, but I am working much harder than I expected." He looks about, unsure of himself.

Then he continues. "I grew up on a kibbutz and it was *yotze min haklal* [extraordinary]. I had none of the worries I have here, you know, rent, school, wages—who needs it? It was a simpler, a happier life."

Many Israelis proclaim their distaste for this country. Even after several years they seem unable to find a niche, to feel comfortable. Often, they maintain primarily Israeli friendships, and they speak Hebrew at every opportunity.

More than anything, they talk of returning. "I'll probably go back in a short time; maybe two years," says the owner of a stereo shop. He was born in Tel Aviv. "I belong there. I can't find myself here. These are just not my people." It is telling that he has been in this country since 1953.

Sami smiles. "We all talk about returning," he confides. "But inside we all know it's a lie. Somebody who wants to return doesn't talk about money or appliances. Could I ever dream about owning a home in Israel?" he asks rhetorically.

His demeanor is matter-of-fact. If he feels any guilt, he isn't showing it. "Look, if I would have remained, I'd have to steal to support my family. It will never be any better over there and we know it, so why should we try to fool people? We aren't fooling ourselves."

II

But if they are unhappy here, if they long to return, then why do they come? The key seems to be in the quaint Israeli colloquialism, lehistader, the term that connotes establishing oneself, setting oneself up.

Lehistader operates in several manners. For most immigrants it is synonymous with economic mobility. Life in Israel means triple-digit inflation, annual reserve military service, and an oppressive tax structure. Yordim are attracted by the promises of prosperity this country has to offer, not unlike millions of other immigrants to these shores.

"Why am I here?" asks Ehud, his thick black hair tousled over his forehead. He and his friends are in their late twenties. "In Israel you can never afford anything. You work hard and you're still broke by the middle of the month. You can never afford to buy an apartment or have a car. I'll make some money and then go back."

There is a sharp exchange in Hebrew between him and his two companions, Zvika and David. "If I could have there what I have here," David smiles, trying to calm himself, "I would run back. My family has been in Jerusalem for more than six generations." He looks up nervously, wondering if that was a smart thing to admit. "I am here two years and what I have earned so far I could never make there in a lifetime."

Zvika, the most emotional of the trio, is losing his patience. "Look," he says, his expression barely concealing a mixture of anger, frustration, and guilt. "I served in two wars, yet I couldn't make a living over there. I can't give all my life. I have to think of myself, too."

His friends try to stop him but he waves them off. "How long can I be an idealist? One, two—five years, maybe. Once in a while you like to have steak for dinner."

The bitterness is not limited to the younger émigrés. Benjamin arrived here about nine years ago, when he was fifty. "Israel always speaks so proudly of its army," he says, his eyes bulging. "So then why don't they take care of their soldiers after they return from the service?"

He is normally a quiet man with a gentle manner. But the distress he feels is very near the surface. He is reflecting his own experiences and those of his children. It isn't easy for him to reconcile the injustice he feels, particularly in light of the love he quickly expresses for his homeland.

"We are proud; we are patriots," he says firmly. "But when a fellow returns after three years in the military, he gets nothing for his time and his sacrifice—no home, no job, no benefits." He is now genuinely agitated.

"All we ever see is that new immigrants get all sorts of benefits," he says, a gloom descending on his brow. "And for what? There is nothing to show our young people that the government appreciates what they have done, nothing to show that they care."

So many come here lehistader. But there is often a surprise in store. There is money to be made here, no doubt. But it requires more effort, more sweat and hard work, than they expected. It is also a different kind of work than they knew before.

Vivian, a pretty, Iraqi-born mother of two, explains, "There is a work ethic here that is missing in Israel. An Israeli here will dump trash for a living six, maybe seven days a week. He'll do work here he would be ashamed to do in Israel. There it is considered better to do no work than to do anything that is demeaning. But not here."

The point rates a smile from Yehuda. Born in Iran, he came to Israel as a teenager and has been in the United States for twenty-six years. A raconteur who loves to talk, Yehuda has seen many of his countrymen come and go. "Israelis come here and work like klavim, like dogs," he says emphatically.

His face exhibits a broad and knowing smile. He is proud of his role as an elder statesman, wise to the ways of the United States.

"Life here is cold and private," he goes on, "so they don't form many relationships. They work harder to try to overcome their insecurities."

He gives a short laugh. "In Israel they wouldn't work as hard because they feel OK." He pauses to reflect on a point he had not anticipated. "It's interesting," he goes on. "Because they have to prove themselves, very few return. You understand, if a fellow is successful, then he'll have to give up too much. If he's a failure, then he's ashamed to go back.

"I'll tell you," he concludes, "life is really getting tough here in the States. The word is getting back. Many of them will think twice before coming in the future."

But lehistader is not just an economic decision. For some it takes cultural and intellectual proportions. Take Yair. "I had a comfortable life in Israel," he says, stretching out on his recliner. In his dark shorts and sandals, he is the model of the native Israeli middle class. "I wrote for a Tel Aviv daily and did public relations work for a large university. Yet I came here several years ago to complete my Ph.D. and to expand my horizons."

He takes a long sip from a frosted glass of ice tea. "It's funny," he says, "when I lived in Israel, I really believed that all those who leave are traitors—you know, yordim. But now I realize that there is a provincial narrow-mindedness. It's difficult to pinpoint. Perhaps it's the tradition, perhaps the political circumstances. Anyway, from America I look at it differently.

Though he expresses the ubiquitous intention to return, Yair feels that he has grown as an individual in ways that could never have been had he stayed in Israel. "America has been very good for me. In Tel Aviv, whenever I met American Jews, even socially—you know, at a party or a cafe—somehow I would always end up fighting with them."

He mimics his old debates. "I'd say, 'what do you understand about life here?' or 'who are you to try and give us advice? You want to be part of the action, then you have to live over here.' That's what I'd tell them."

He seems a bit sheepish about it all, even now. "I was always defensive. I guess I reflected the insecurities of my environment." He laughs. "The ironic part is that I got away with it, even among Americans. You know, I was a *sabra* [native-born Israeli]—aggressive and arrogant. Over here I learned that humility is also a virtue."

III

However one chooses to interpret lehistader, Israeli émigrés appear to have much in common. Anxious to achieve material wealth, many are prepared to sacrifice their cultural heritage in its name. They consume as conspicuously as any American, with a fondness for gadgetry as their trademark.

Yair theorizes about the point. "In Israel," he says loudly, forcefully, "we were poor, frustrated capitalists. We had aspirations, but we hid behind socialism. You must understand that our socialism is a bastard born of poverty rather than ideology."

He waves at his nicely furnished apartment, replete with color television, video cassette recorder, and stereo. "To make others jealous, *lenaker eynayim*, has always been part of our culture. As a result, Israelis here try to accumulate as much as they can. They become more materialistic than the Americans." And in this, they are not distinguishable from most other recent immigrants to these shores.

Interestingly, some yordim have reinforced their ties to Judaism since coming to the United States, even the most secular among them. But the response is neither ritual nor theological. In fact, most are quick to explain that they feel uncomfortable in U.S. synagogues. Instead, they see their Jewish identity as a link homeward. Even the least prayerful seem more sympathetic to Jewish observance than they ever were before. Says Rena, a striking twenty-four-year-old of Yemenite birth: "In Israel we were quite irreligious. My husband worked on Shabbat; we needed the money!"

She goes on. "Here we are closer to religion. Not observant, really, but, for instance, I light candles on Friday night and I cry when I attend the synagogue. Not my husband," she laughs and throws up her hands is desperation, "he still won't go."

Her friend Vivian nods in agreement. "I go to the synagogue on Shabbat and holidays so that my children won't forget that they are Israelis. Even though we speak Hebrew at home," she frowns, "I see them forgetting."

Suddenly she turns reflective. "Religion in Israel is a caricature. The religious organizations are their own worst enemies. We used to laugh at them. Still, in Israel, religious or not, you know it's Shabbat."

In the same breath as they express their longing to return to Israel, many yordim also reflect disaffection and anger over specific aspects of life in their homeland. Perhaps these are retrospective; perhaps they would not be sufficient cause to leave. But the scars are there, very close to the surface. Listen to Chaim: "Army service is a sham," he says, his voice rising with each sentence. Chaim is a diamond cutter, who arrived here from Jerusalem about eight years ago. "No matter what they tell you, not everyone is subject. I remember once, I got back from my reserve tour—up in the Golan for three months—and my friends laughed at me. Talk to so-and-so, they told me, and you could have avoided the whole damn thing."

Not surprisingly, their loudest scowls are reserved for those high-level Israeli officials who have railed against them from their government perches. They take particular pleasure in reports of government scandal and official misconduct. It is a vindication for their argument that the entire establishment is rife with corruption. That those on top criticize private citizens for personal decisions is pure hypocrisy!

Particular targets for their disdain are the various consular officials and *shlichim*, government or party representatives in the United States. Rather than treat their citizens with respect, Israelis claim, members of the diplomatic corps think that they have uniformed troops at their command. Why can't our embassy treat us as Americans are treated by theirs in a foreign country?

Perhaps the Israeli diplomatic corps and its foreign service are too heavy with retired military personnel and party hacks. An assignment in the United States is a much sought political plum, given as reward for loyal service and seniority (read patience) to many who are unqualified and inexperienced. It's an opportunity to gain some publicity, to lecture, to make a bit of money—in short, lehistader. You see, everybody does it.

"These people are *pesulim*, you know, worthless," Benjamin chimes in. His assessment is harsh. Yet it reflects much of what his compatriots really feel. "They look out for themselves. They're here to have a good time. I wonder how many remain after their tour is completed. How many become yordim themselves."

Yair agrees. He places his thinking on psychological grounds. "I believe the Israeli government really wants us to return. But they are making a mistake. Look," he says, a bit annoyed, "If somebody calls me a son-of-bitch, then whatever guilt I may have felt about being here is dissipated. I can feel no obligation toward someone who insults me publicly."

IV

What Israelis are most unhappy about in the United States is the way that they are "forced" to rear their children here and the way their children—be they preschoolers or adolescents—are affected. They call this a "prison for children" where kids must sit in front of a television, locked in an apartment all day. Despite the economic and social hardships of their homeland, they consider it ideal for raising children. There they are surrounded by warm and friendly neighbors, the freedom to wander about as they please, and the honest values of Israeli life. They can't help but grow up successfully.

Yosef, an official with an Israeli government agency whom I met at his home, put it succinctly. "Children here are hostage to their environment. We can't send our kids to their friends alone. In Israel this would be incredible. We have always taught our children to be unafraid." He stands, walks to the refrigerator, and returns with a container in his hand.

"Look," he says, pointing to the face of a missing child on the milk carton. "In Israel we send our children among Arab workers, and we are never afraid of this sort of thing happening. Believe me," he pauses to calm himself, "the good life that Israelis may have here doesn't make up for the freedom of their children." But there is something more bothering him. Surely, there are inherent dangers in raising children where terrorists plant bombs in parked cars and attack commuter buses. What about the high rate of fatalities among Israeli drivers and pedestrians?

Then the scene shifts. "There is also something very different about the mentality of the Jew in *galut*, in the Diaspora, especially here in the States," he begins slowly, carefully choosing his words.

"We were here for no more than six months before my five-year-old started singing Christmas songs. But really that wasn't so bad. It was the other American Jews who disturbed me the most." He looks up, a pained expression crossing his face.

"I suppose it was the hypocrisy of having my son in a parochial school class where children were taught to lie about their home lives and outside activities." His words are no longer measured. Anger and frustration are close to the surface now.

"Look," he continued, "all the children know who eats at Mc-Donald's or Burger King, you know, not kosher. But they all promise that they don't do it. My kid learned that to get along here, he didn't have to give up anything; he just had to lie like all the other kids. In Israel this would never happen."

While most Israeli parents are less philosophical about their children, they have the same misgivings, misgivings which speak right to the ambivalence that they feel themselves. In the words of one young father: "You know what you should call this [chapter]? 'Schizophrenia!' " His wife is quick to intercede, trying to soften the blow. "Look," she explains, "identity is the real issue here. Our kids may not realize it, but they don't know who they are. They are being brought up without a homeland. Other Jews won't accept us here, so naturally we're a little cliquish. They think that a good Israeli is one who fights for them in the Middle East. I don't have to justify my being here!" The delivery of her last words is anything but soft.

"So now look at our children," she goes on, a bit more composed. "My son is dressed well; he dreams about a puppy or a ten-speed. In Israel, kids his age are already talking about which brigade they will enter and what will be their specialty in the military."

She pauses for a moment. She is collecting her thoughts, but a small sigh escapes as well. Her head turns away. "What does he know about the army? He shivers whenever we mention it. Really, we'll never tell him, but . . . it makes us ashamed."

It's much too easy, however, to confuse what the children actually feel and what their parents project upon them. Though unintended, her point may well be that children feel far less sharply the guilt and shame of their parents. That makes their parents feel still more guilty and ashamed. So we must get to know the children as well.

Listen to Eynat, for example, a blond twelve-year-old with a bright smile. "I don't know, it's just that in Israel people are friendlier. Here the first thing they do is criticize. Israelis look on the good side. You know . . . " a pained expression shadows her face as she searches for the right word. "It's like . . . they start off being your friend."

Nati agrees. He is sharp and articulate, with a devilish expression on his face. "I think that Americans take friendship too lightly," he says, reflecting an insight far beyond his meager ten years. "They

break friendships very easily. Maybe that's why most of our friends
and our parents' friends are also Israelis.''

"That's really true," says Tamar, who at eleven has spent virtually
all her life in the United States. "Whenever we visit Israel, I have a
lot of fun. It's easier to make friends there, like on the first day.
Sometimes they tease me about my accent. Or if I drink soda from a
straw, they say I'm a typical American, but it's just easier there.''

The children ramble on about their friends, parents, and school, just
like any other kids. They speak freely, confidently, though their mothers are sitting right there. In many ways they are typical suburban
kids—designer shirts, jeans, multicolored running shoes, and all. There
really isn't anything to distinguish them, to remind one that they are
different. But they think they are.

"Also, I think that our parents are different from the others," says
Yuval thoughtfully. He was born in the United States and he has moved
from California to New York. "They're hardworking people who care
more for their children." Eynat jumps in, not allowing him to finish
his thought. There is a jumble of Hebrew as her mother scolds her for
being rude, but she goes on anyway.

"My friends' mothers are 'microwave' types,'' she says, and they
all giggle. "You know, they don't care as much about their children.
They let them go to town or to the movies alone." She takes a breath
and giggles again. "Also, they wear sweatsuits and punk sun glasses,
like a kid—not like a mother.''

More cross fire between parents and children. Then Eynat continues. "Sometimes my father embarrasses me, though. He always tries
to be friendly, you know, like talking to people he doesn't even know.''
More giggles. "I try to explain to him, that's not the way in America.
Here parents are more detached; they're not so involved.''

I look at the faces of these youngsters and ponder all that I have
been told about them and their parents. Eynat interrupts my musings.
"Actually, I've always felt a little uncomfortable here. I wanted to go
to public school and be like other American kids. But . . . I still want
to keep my own personality.''

Nati picks it up. "For a while, I changed my name to Andrew. No
real reason. I just liked Andrew." The others laugh and he turns a bit
red. "But you know, it didn't help, so I went back to Nati.''

Eynat hasn't lost her train of thought. She goes on, ignoring the
others. "Every year my parents promise that we're going back, we're

going back, but it doesn't happen. Either let's do it or let's forget about it.'' She looks at her mother and then away, nervously. "Pretty soon I'll be old enough and I'll just go back on my own!''

Her comment elicits a sharp reaction from the adults in the room. There is a loud exchange in rapid-fire Hebrew. She just looks at me and smiles.

V

If identity is the major issue, both for children and for their parents, some Israelis have tried to do something about it. Both independently and with the assistance of various institutions in this country, they have created a variety of clubs, organizations, and supplementary school programs for their children. These go by such expressive titles as Ha-tzofim (the scouts), Keshet va-hetz (bow and arrow), and Etgar (the challenge).

Ostensibly these programs were established to prepare these children for their return to Israel. As one mother put it: "We don't want them to forget their language and the love they must have for their land. When they return, we want them to fit.'' But in a short while, it became evident that other functions were also being performed by these new incarnations.

In the first instance, sending their kids to these schools and youth programs gives Israelis here a sense of belonging that they never felt within organizations dominated by U.S. Jews. It offers them the opportunity to reminisce, to meet, and to socialize. Perhaps most of all, it allows them a further outlet for their almost obsessive drive to speak Hebrew.

In addition, it's no secret that the large majority of Israelis in this country will never return. Programs such as these offer them a taste of the "old country,'' helping to assuage the conscience some. At least they are encouraging their children to learn something of the mother tongue and culture. In this regard, they are no different from most immigrants anywhere.

The point is driven home by a visit to Gahelet (the glowing ember), a twice-weekly program for Israeli children, operating within the religious school of Temple Israel of Great Neck, New York. There are over eighty children at Gahelet, ranging from kindergarten to eighth grade. The school's leadership prides itself on the similarity between

its offerings and the Israeli public school curriculum. Teachers are all
recent arrivals who hold Israeli certification. Emphasis is placed upon
Bible (taught from a secular literary and historical perspective), current events in Israel, and written composition. Then there is Moledet.

A loosely designed combination of geography, civics, and map study,
Moledet is intended to inspire an appreciation for the topography and
natural beauty of Israel. It also seems to fulfill a need within the parents. "One of the things I really miss," says one young mother as we
wait for her daughter to be dismissed, "is *nof*, the landscape. You just
don't get that here."

Of course, all instruction takes place in Hebrew. If there is one
overriding objective for these children, it is to renew and reinforce
their Hebrew fluency. Ironically, some of them have been in the United
States most of their lives; others were born here. Indeed, this is also
one of the attractions for Temple Israel, according to Rabbi Marim
Charry, its educational director. "We are very happy to have a He-
brew-speaking presence in our midst," he explains from behind a desk
heavy with papers, books, and files.

"We have a lot to learn about each other," he smiles. There are
differences, for example, over religious standards as well as the matter
of decorum. Israeli kids "are not a controlled group," Charry explains, "and the parents don't see it as a problem. They say that's the
way Israelis are."

The leadership of Gahelet offers another perspective, however, at a
parents' meeting in the synagogue. They are indeed a lively group,
with much socializing both before and during the program. Shouts of
"Hi, *mah nishma*? What's up?" abound in all directions.

The attendance is marked by designer clothes and careful manicures
as well as torn jeans and gritty hands. This is a group of mixed socioeconomic status held together largely by its ethnic identity. They all
appear genuinely concerned about the future of Gahelet.

"This has been a very successful year," says Ruti, the administrator of the program and a parent herself. The dual designation is not
unusual here. She is trying to bring the sizable group to order, but
there is an undercurrent of chatter throughout. It doesn't appear to
bother her; she is accustomed to it.

"And the major reason for our success," she continues, "is the *S*
with two lines. That's what Americans understand! We brought in

quite a lot of money to the school, and they realize that we're not just a bunch of Israeli 'schleppers' [ne'er-do-wells].''

In private conversation, Ruti expands her thoughts. ''The temple has been very good to us,'' she says slowly, ''better than could be expected. But we have tried to return some of that as well. We have a holiday '*hagigah*' with a performance and lots of singing, like on Purim, and our people really turn out. Yom Haatzmaut was a high point.'' She is proud of Gahelet and gratified that it could carry its own weight.

''The parents are a major part of our success,'' she explains. ''They participate, really take an active role. We tell them that they can't just drop the kids off two days a week. They have to work with the kids and be in touch with the teachers. This is really much more serious than the usual Hebrew school.''

Informal conversation with the parents confirms these thoughts. It also confirms that programs like Gahelet serve the needs of the adults as much as those of the children, and that is the real key to their success.

VI

Is there no middle ground here? Can Israel come to terms with a steady out-migration of a variety of its citizens? Or will its formal stance continue to alienate those who have left and encourage others lehistader? Will their guilt and confusion simply dissipate with time? Or can a constructive note be struck, one that might encourage some to return and others to serve Israel's needs from these shores?

The issues are complicated, and Israeli officialdom is of many minds. The more harsh have already been documented. But the responses of some Israeli representatives in the United States are surprisingly optimistic. Take Moshe, a ranking official of the Jewish Agency whose primary responsibility is immigration and settlement.

''We cannot legitimate their being here,'' he says slowly. ''We will not help them build an establishment here. The place for Israelis is Israel,'' he adds emphatically, ''and we look upon their stay here as temporary.''

He speaks proudly of the variety of services and benefits made available to help Israelis here maintain a link with their homeland and ease their passage back. He displays pamphlets in Hebrew that speak of favorable mortgage terms and tax-free status for purchase of appliances, all available to those who would return.

"We wish to give them rights as Israelis, yet all the benefits of a new immigrant," he says warmly. "We need them and we are waiting for them." His closing words are almost a plea. They are echoed by the full-color brochures that seem to call out to the yored: "Come home! Bring your VCRs, your stereos, and your newfound horizons, but for God's sake, come home!"

They are also echoed by Uri, an agency colleague involved with public relations. "Israel cannot accept emigration," he says firmly. "We find it difficult even to understand it. It is against our Zionist upbringing, it is against our culture—it is against everything we have come to know and desire." A soft-spoken reserve officer of Iraqi birth, he speaks at length of the dedication of Israelis, even while in the United States. "Otherwise, why would they rush home at the first sign of war?" he exclaims. "All our reservists, all of them, came home to fight. Unfortunately, they left when the war ended."

Then Uri shifts gears. He becomes romantic, almost mystical. "There is a change in the atmosphere in Israel," he declares. "People will much more readily accept one who returns. Much of their bitterness is gone and has been replaced by understanding."

He looks into space. "Perhaps wandering is part of being Jewish. Moving from place to place has crept into our genes, and most Israeli residents understand this very well."

But a less optimistic note is struck by Uzi, a representative of the Israel consulate in New York, the area that seems to have attracted the lion's share of yordim. "We want to see them back in Israel," he agrees, a smile on his face as of to emphasize the obvious. "They are part of us and we need them."

He concedes that the various economic programs and material incentives have not been particularly successful. In addition, he notes that there are still many in Israel who take a dim view of emigration.

"Look, in many ways, Israel is a battlefield, and someone who leaves it will be seen by many as a deserter. I think that the government is trying to be more sympathetic now," he says slowly. "But it's hard to change people's views about a subject like this."

But does it make any more sense to try to bribe yordim than it does to insult them? Israel cannot compete with the United States financially, and few Israelis will return for material reasons. To the contrary, emphasizing the material may just reinforce their resolve to stay.

What of the frustrations of those who never left? How are they to understand a program that rewards those who emigrate and return with special benefits and allowances? Won't that just encourage them to "play the yored game," that is, leave Israel, make some money, and then claim a desire to return? Then they would arrive back in Israel with government blessing and a slew of material advantages and credits.

"I don't agree with this policy," mutters a lower-level employee at the Jewish Agency. "Living in Israel is a privilege. In America kids are raised by standards that are unacceptable in Israel. There, kids are healthier physically, spiritually, and emotionally. These are the things we should emphasize.

"No yored is happy with his family and social life here. He misses the freedom, the security, and the climate of his home. It's here that we can compete with America, and these are the things that should appear in our literature. The potential to attract yordim exists, but between the insults and the bribery, we're going to lose these people and thousands more."

Back at Sami's café, I ponder these thoughts as I munch on my pita. Sami brings my coffee and sits down next to me. "See that couple over there?" he says, pointing to two people at the next table. "They are here five years and still can't find themselves. David is very happy here, or so he says. Rena is always crying about her home and family in Israel."

They have been talking loudly through their meal, but I've paid little attention. Now I listen more carefully. Their words seem to present the issue in microcosm. The guilt, the frustration, the bitterness—it's all there. Witness:

"I feel like a traitor," Rena complains. "I'm ashamed to admit that I'm an Israeli—the mere word makes me feel like a deserter. This is not my land. What am I doing here? I have abandoned my people."

"Who have you deserted?" David answers angrily. "Peres, Rabin, and the rest? Don't be absurd! They don't care about you. Don't talk like a fool! I do what is best for me and my family—I'm no Zionist."

"I'm sorry, it hurts every time I walk into a store and I hear Hebrew, or I see children running around with a *kova tembil* [Israeli cap]. The weather, the land—it just isn't mine."

"What do you want? We have a TV, a washer, a dryer, a stereo. We eat out twice a week. Did you ever have these things over there? If you're such a patriot, why don't you wear a blue and white flag?"

At this point Rena bursts into tears. David does not seem impressed. No doubt this is a scene he has witnessed before. Panting, almost unable to speak she blurts: "You are talking about politics and money, but I am talking about my life. My life is over there!"

10

Whither Soviet Jewry?

I

It is now almost two decades since the plight of Soviet Jews became an issue of major concern for Israel and the Jewish communities of the West. Their fortunes have waxed during the heyday of Soviet-U.S. détente and the promise of increased trade between the two giants. They have waned in the aftermath of the Soviet invasion of Afghanistan, the fall of the Shah, and the rise of Ronald Reagan.

In general, the exodus of Jews from the Soviet Union has been captive to international diplomacy and the mazes that are Soviet internal affairs and U.S. foreign policy. With it has gone the morale of those who organize to do battle on their behalf. It has been a dizzying journey fraught with confusion and conflict, both internal and external. Even after twenty years, many of the same personalities are still arguing the same issues.

Objective analysis is difficult, and reliable figures are hard to come by.* The Soviets officially estimate that there are about 1.8 million

This chapter is an expanded and updated version of "Soviet Jewry: Malaise in The Movement," originally published in *Midstream*, March 1980.

*Most of the data cited here are based upon those collected by the National Conference on Soviet Jewry and the Greater New York Conference on Soviet Jewry from both Soviet and independent sources. See, for example, *Soviet Jewry: Fact and Fiction* (New York: National Conference on Soviet Jewry, 1986).

Jews in the Soviet Union, about 70 percent of whom reside in the Russian Republic or the Ukraine. As has been their history throughout most of Europe, the Jews of the Soviet Union tend to concentrate in or near the big cities. These data suggest a decline of almost 25 percent over the past generation. In varying degrees the drop is due to emigration, low birth rates, and high rates of intermarriage. Still, their numbers rank them as the third largest Jewish community in the world, after the United States and Israel.

For reasons that are far from clear, Soviet Jews experienced a renewal of Jewish identity during the late 1960s. Some attribute it to Israel's dramatic victories during the 1967 Six Day War. To be sure, only sketchy and inaccurate reports filtered through Soviet censorship, but it was enough to spur a reawakening of pride and interest in things Jewish. The renewal was most evident in regard to identifications with Zionism and the State of Israel.

Not discounting the 1967 War and its impact, what took place may have also been closely related to internal Soviet policy. In one formulation, then Soviet leader Leonid Brezhnev saw the release of a handful of chronic Jewish malcontents as an opportunity to relieve dissident pressures. His primary concern was to rid the country of a few troublemakers, but he also hoped the move would be interpreted as a humanitarian gesture. Its result could lead to U.S. concessions in trade as well as big power détente. These two issues would return to haunt the Soviets in the years that followed, as the movement was not mollified but rather grew with the release of these early dissidents.

Yet another scenario suggests that Jewish activism in the Soviet Union was the result of Soviet social policies. In order to integrate native elites from the several Soviet nationalities, the leadership found it necessary to open opportunities for them at universities and to place them after graduation. Given the disproportionate presence of Jews in academia and the professions during the 1950s and 1960s, these new social developments hit them especially hard. Quotas were imposed that made life in the Soviet Union especially difficult for Jews. Soviet figures suggest that the proportion of Jews among scientific workers has declined by some 67 percent over the past thirty years. Similarly, Jewish enrollment in programs of higher education in the city of Moscow declined by about 50 percent from 1970 to 1980. To be sure, the long history of Soviet anti-Semitism made the task of excluding Jews not altogether unpleasant for Soviet officials.

Whether an increase in Jewish affiliation and identity among Soviet Jews was the result of positive or reactive energies, it is clear that the late 1960s was a turning point for them. What began as a small trickle soon became a mass movement both within the Soviet Union and abroad, including dissidents and supporters among Jews and Gentiles alike.

Generally, the first few Jews allowed to leave were able to make some humanitarian claim based on the desire to be reunited with close relatives, generally in Israel. The Soviets could allow them to leave without conceding anything about conditions in their proletarian paradise. But the decision was soon to become table stakes at the game of international diplomacy.

During the early 1970s, the Soviet Union made overtures toward the United States. They sought both détente and, especially, favorable trade concessions in the form of most favored nation (MFN) status. This would allow the United States and the Soviet Union to increase trade by reducing many of the tariffs and restrictions that would otherwise exist.

Primarily, the Soviets hoped to import large amounts of grain. In addition, they indicated interest in our computer and aerospace industries as well as other high-tech products. Further down the road, they believed that many of their own products, notably vodka, cars, and tractors, might be competitively marketed in the United States.

For all of the reasons listed above, Soviet leaders chose to emphasize their desire for détente and warm the waters of trade between the great powers. As a corollary, they permitted some seventy-five thousand Soviet Jewish dissidents to emigrate during 1972–73. These were primarily refuseniks, a term designating those who had requested permission to leave but were refused and who often suffered personal and professional hardship as a result of their applications.

The U.S. Congress responded quite differently. Encouraged by leaders of the Soviet Jewry movement as well as by U.S. Jewish leaders generally (who for the most part were one and the same), they did not take the Soviet move as an expression of good will and instead chose to use Soviet political and economic needs as a prod to encourage increased emigration and to loosen restrictions on human rights. Put cynically, it would be Jews for trade.

The result was embodied in the Trade Act of 1974. An amendment cosponsored by Sen. Henry Jackson (D-Wash.) and Rep. Charles Vanik (D-Ohio) placed a special burden on trading partners who lacked a market economy, that is, Communist states. In return for most favored nation status, they had to provide assurances that they would extend basic civil rights to their citizens, including the right to emigrate. A later addition by Sen. Adlai Stevenson (D-Ill.) severely restricted financial credits for countries exhibiting a poor record on human rights.

The term *assurances* in the legislation was never clearly defined, and a series of compromises soon was offered to soften the language. Lengthy negotiations ensued between Congress and the administration as well as between the U.S. State Department and representatives of the Soviet Union. Moscow ultimately rejected the pact as a crude attempt by a foreign power to dictate domestic policy. Surely, Soviet leaders argued, the United States, given its own record of racial injustice and discrimination, was hardly in a position to lecture others regarding human rights. In addition, linking trade to Jewish rights would never reduce restrictions on emigration policy. On the contrary, they claimed (or threatened) that it would actually increase anti-Semitism, presumably both popular and official.

What remained was a bit of hard-line legislation that virtually excluded all socialist countries from MFN status. It was softened only by provisions for a twelve-month waiver should the president receive adequate assurances of compliance on questions of human rights. Though the Soviet Union rejected the formulation, it was hailed by the bulk of the Soviet Jewry movement as a major victory.

II

The years that followed Jackson-Vanik offered both dismay and encouragement. On the one hand, the Soviets were true to their threat. In reaction to the arrogance that they perceived in U.S. trade policy, the numbers of Soviet Jews allowed to leave was curtailed. As mentioned earlier, during the two years prior to the legislation (1972–73), about seventy-five thousand Jews had been permitted to emigrate, perhaps in response to the Strategic Arms Limitation Talks (SALT) agreement and the first big grain arrangements. That was about 10,000 more than were granted exit visas for the four years following Jackson-Vanik, 1974 through 1977.

On the other hand, two other East European Communist countries did manage to qualify under the legislation. An increase in exit visas and a reduction in related harassment won most favored nation status for Rumania in 1975 and for Hungary in 1978. Assurances were forthcoming either through direct statements regarding human rights or by an exchange of correspondence carefully worded to soften the perception of foreign interference. Apparently, international trade could be carried on in the context of Jackson-Vanik.

As already noted, cause and effect are difficult to define in Soviet politics. Perhaps allowing these two clients to enter into an agreement with the United States was simply Moscow's way of testing the waters of international trade. Alternatively, Soviet reactions may actually have been inspired by the independent decisions of these Warsaw Pact allies.

At the same time, the United States was exploiting the "China card"—an attempt to warm relations with the Oriental giant who was also seeking trade concessions and the import of U.S. technology. The Soviets grew alarmed at the increasingly cozy relationship between the United States and the People's Republic, its primary adversary in the Communist world. It feared the development of a United States-China-Japan axis; "encirclement," they called it.

For any or all of these reasons, the level of Soviet Jewish emigration rose dramatically in the late 1970s. Some thirty thousand were permitted to leave in 1978, and over fifty-one thousand left in 1979. It was a record high that stands to this day.

Yet the matter of MFN for the Soviet Union would have to be handled very delicately. Increased emigration was fine and good, but what of assurances? The Soviet Union was neither Rumania nor Hungary. Superficial face-saving devices would never do for a nation jealous of its status as a superpower equal to the United States.

The debate that raged over these and related issues was soon to become moot. In quick succession, the Shah of Iran fell, the Soviet Union invaded Afghanistan, and Ronald Reagan was elected president of the United States. These events all signaled a sharp change in U.S.-Soviet relations, at least for the near term. U.S. foreign policy in Europe, the Middle East, and the Mediterranean regions would have to be evaluated anew in the context of Reagan's tough and moralistic vision of international affairs.

What followed was a precipitous reduction in Jewish emigration from the Soviet Union as the superpowers eyed each other suspiciously from a distance. Far from the record numbers of 1979, fewer than ten thousand Jews left the Soviet Union in 1981, and fewer than one thousand were permitted exit in 1984. For any who still harbored doubt, it was painfully clear that the right to emigrate was fully subject to Soviet-U.S. relations. The issue was not high on either nation's agenda.

So the movement languished for most of Reagan's first administration. It was a period of fiscal retrenchment, high unemployment, and economic redirection for the United States. Always closer to the hearts of U.S. voters, these issues took much of the political focus away from the international arena.

By the same token, the Soviet Union experienced a crisis of leadership. Old and isolated from the popular beat, the Soviet oligarchy underwent confusion and discord as Brezhnev gave way to Andropov and then to Chernenko. In periods of fear and uncertainty, it is not uncommon for totalitarian systems to turn inward, to allow old suspicions and prejudices to take grip, and to exhibit political paralysis. The Soviet Union was no exception. Suffice it to say that it was not a time for bold new international initiatives.

Ronald Reagan's second election to the presidency in 1984 and the rise of Mikhail Gorbachev as general secretary of the Soviet Union ushered in what became known as "the thaw of '85." Gorbachev, a relatively young, cosmopolitan figure, signaled that his administration might be marked by a new period in U.S.-Soviet relations.

Anxious to add a major foreign policy victory to his arsenal of domestic accomplishments, President Reagan seized the moment. Within the year, U.S.-Soviet arms reduction talks were opened, and the two leaders held a summit conference in Geneva. It was essential to Western Jewish leaders that there be no trade and no détente without consideration of human rights and the plight of refuseniks. If they could help it, Soviet Jewry was to be on the diplomatic table once more.

At least at first, accomplishments were limited to the splashy and the spectacular. Instead of indicating goodwill through high emigration figures, new Soviet leaders ignored the rank-in-file and reached for individual celebrities of the dissident movement, both Jewish and gentile.

From 1984 to 1986, for example, such fathers of Soviet protest as Anatoly Shcharansky, Yosef Mendelevich, Elia Esses, and Yuri Orlov were permitted to leave the Soviet Union. In addition, Yelena Bonner, wife of Soviet grand dissident Andrei Sakharov, was allowed to travel to the West for medical treatment, providing she made no public statements of political or diplomatic consequence.

The sensational results of these new Soviet-U.S. initiatives electrified Western leaders of the Soviet Jewry movement. They also reintroduced confusions and tensions that had not been confronted for years. Questions of priority, tactics, and strategy were reopened. Many of the rifts that had been carefully papered over during the bad times of the early 1980s were uncovered. There were also new players on the scene, with new demands, new stakes, and new constituencies.

Essentially, the challenge has three facets. One is social, having to do with patterns of emigration and the settlement of new Soviet Jewish arrivals. It is a challenge that, at some levels, pits Jewish commitment to Israel against the desire to free their brethren from the Soviet regime.

A second is political and economic. We have already demonstrated the implicit and explicit links enacted between Soviet emigration policy and trade relations with the United States. There is contemporary, yet familiar, debate regarding appropriate strategies for new trade and security arrangements between the United States and the Soviet Union, given the long-standing provisions of Jackson-Vanik.

The third, a new wrinkle on the international brow, is diplomatic. The Soviet Union has recently made overtures toward Israel regarding the renewal of ties broken after the 1967 War. Because Israel is an advocate for Jewish rights internationally, the extent of Israel's determination to win concessions regarding Soviet emigration policy has been linked to this development. It is a matter of concern both within its borders and beyond.

III

Regarding patterns of emigration, the heart of the matter is the simple fact that support for Soviet Jewry was originally conceived as an aliyah movement. It was to be a program that would aid both Israel and the Jews of the Soviet Union by providing a pool of motivated and talented new immigrants for the former and by working to secure the right of exit for the latter. Indeed, visas issued to Soviet Jews generally declare Israel as their destination, after necessary stopovers in Europe.

But a funny thing happens on the way to Tel Aviv. During their brief hiatus at immigrant centers in Rome, Vienna, and elsewhere, large percentages of newly liberated émigrés alter their visas and their

choices of residence. For example, roughly 265,000 Jews left the Soviet Union from 1968 to the end of 1985, but by the most generous
estimates only some 170,000 of them presently reside in Israel. Others
suggest that the figure may be as low as 140,000.

Of the remainder, about 100,000 came to the United States. Sizable
contingents also left for Australia and Canada. In the heady days of
the late 1970s, only about 34 percent of Soviet emigrants arrived in
Israel. In the absence of reliable figures, it appears that even among
those who do go to Israel initially, many leave after a short stay—
mainly for the United States. In sum, the movement to gain freedom
for Soviet Jewry can no longer be portrayed as an aliyah enterprise.

There are two schools of thought in this regard. For many, it is no
cause for concern. No matter what their destination, they argue, the
Jews of the Soviet Union are our brothers and sisters in need. There
is a real obligation on the part of Jews in the free world to alleviate
their pain. The obligation simply demands that they be assisted by any
means possible in their justifiable desire to leave the Soviet Union.
Attempting to structure or limit their choice of destination is just a
further denial of freedom. It is ill advised for those whose rhetoric
links the plight of Soviet Jews to the international movement for human rights and the Helsinki Accords.

The argument has a particular sting to it. Is it not hypocritical for
those who reside in New York, Chicago, Boston, or Los Angeles to
be concerned over the unwillingness of many Soviet Jews to live in
Israel? Economic concerns, as well as those of culture and security,
have always intervened in U.S. Zionist aspirations. Large numbers of
Israelis have shown an equal affinity for this golden land. Why should
we expect otherwise of these newly liberated Jews who have had far
less exposure to Judaism or Zionism for most of their lives?

There is a highly emotional theme underlying it all. During World
War II, it is claimed, Zionist groups, making impossible decisions
under extreme conditions, followed similar lines in working with refugees from war-ravaged Europe. Card-carrying members of Zionist
organizations were given priority, as were those who proclaimed the
willingness to live in Palestine.

It is a dark accusation that crops up now and again in the most
unlikely quarters, and it is one that invariably meets with harsh and
often violent response. Aside from any intended aspersions, the lesson
is clear. Whether out of religious commitment, fraternal loyalty, or

simple humanism, Jews must be aided in their quest to leave the Soviet Union, no matter what their intended destination.

But there are those who object for reasons that are more subtle and less emotional but equally compelling. First, the large number of dropouts, *noshrim*, as they are known in Hebrew, do Israel an injustice. For some, Israel's well-being transcends the Soviet Jewry issue at all points.

Sorely in need of friends and sporting an injured public image in the wake of the Lebanese campaign, Israel does not need the specter of Soviet Jews, painted as activists desiring to be reunited with their people, turning their collective backs and heading for the affluent U.S. shores. Editorially, those arriving in the United States have more than occasionally offered unkind assessments of Jewish commitments and Zionism. While explanations for their unseemly behavior abound, the cut has left its mark.

Though the bulk of U.S. Jewish society has been Zionized, divisions over the matter of noshrim have often followed classic lines. The resulting splits between and among Jewish organizations reveal the battle scars of another era. To be sure, having to choose between the priority of Israel or Soviet Jewry is both painful and unfair, yet those organizations who identify themselves as primarily Zionist tend to choose differently from those who view their function more in terms of defense, civil rights, or communal relations.

Then there are the immigrants themselves. Perhaps it is simple naiveté, or perhaps there is a natural tendency for activists to believe their own press releases. Regardless, Soviet Jews arriving in the United States have not always made a favorable impression upon those who consider themselves to be benefactors.

Neither impoverished and deferential nor militant and proud, most émigrés appear to be educated, moderately affluent, and primarily motivated by hopes of economic mobility. Distant from Judaism, they display little of the commitment to ritual and culture that has been part of the movement's rhetoric from the first. Harshly conditioned toward suspicion and mistrust as a way of life, they are naturally hesitant to join in public programs or to share their experiences and emotions in communal solidarity and activism.

For their part, the immigrants come from a paternalistic society that offered them broad-based, though somewhat meager, economic security. They arrive with what some agencies call an "entitlement men-

tality.'' Expecting quick economic mobility and affluence, it is often
difficult for them to adapt to a culture that prizes independence and
initiative.

Not infrequently, there is tension and misunderstanding on both sides.
Local leaders cannot understand the reluctance of "their Russians" to
join in holiday services, send their children to Hebrew schools, and
participate in all manner of communal activities. Immigrants cannot
fathom disappointment displayed at their desire to land jobs commen-
surate with their training, and they seem unable to be sufficiently grateful
to virtually everyone they meet.

As with any large migration, this one also displays its share of pa-
thologies. Law enforcement authorities already speak of a ''Russian
Mafia,'' émigré criminal gangs involved with fraud, extortion, and
counterfeiting. The result has often erupted into street violence, frequently victimizing other immigrants. In addition, security services are
concerned that among these former Soviet citizens are KGB contacts.
The brighter and better educated, it is feared, are targeted to gain
citizenship and rise into sensitive positions in government, industry,
and academia.

It is also demoralizing for U.S. activists to be reminded that, at least
indirectly, they contributed to the problem. To be sure, the Israeli
Foreign Office provides the necessary documentation, but Soviet Jews
have always been umbilically linked to their U.S. supporters through
personal letters, highly publicized protests and campaigns, as well as
interventions with U.S. public officials up to the president himself.

Perhaps the problem is rooted in a simple fact. The movement has
always seen itself as an exciting and highly visible enterprise in human
rights advocacy, but it has also taken on certain aspects of immigrant
aid and settlement, a much less romantic and adventurous predisposi-
tion. In the words of one local activist from the Midwest: "I would
hate to think that the result of my involvement, protest, and even ar-
rest was just so that some junior-grade engineer from Kiev could get
a better job in Chicago.''

IV

Migration patterns aside, debates over present political strategy center around the leaner days of 1986–87, days in which Jewish emigration from the Soviet Union has been at its lowest. The suggestions of

a warmer relationship between the superpowers has given new hope that trends of the recent past might be reversed. The hope has also spawned confusion and conflict within the movement and has produced two distinct camps.

There are the hardliners, those who believe that the best interests of Soviet Jews are served by strict adherence to the letter of Jackson-Vanik. A tough stance, they argue, one predicated upon a continued link of trade and détente with human rights policy, is the only kind of language the Soviets understand. Approaching them piecemeal, offering the names of individual activists to be released, abandons the advantage. All that remains is purely humanitarian, and that is something they won't respect and can ignore with impunity. At best it smacks of tokenism.

Besides, the Soviet Union has indicated its abiding interest in U.S. agricultural technology, computers, and sophisticated oil-drilling equipment. The time is ripe to make them understand that a warming of commercial and diplomatic relations will require an atmosphere of trust and good will. Soviet Jewry is precisely the barometer issue on which they can forge a new relationship. It would be criminal for the movement to buckle at this most portentous moment.

Others are a bit more circumspect. Perhaps Jackson-Vanik has been improperly untilized in the past, they suggest. It is, after all, merely a tool, not an end in itself. It serves neither the needs of Soviet Jewry nor of U.S. foreign policy to club Moscow with it or to raise it to a symbolic level for which it was never intended.

Might it be, they continue, that the Soviets tired of currying favor with the West in the late 1970s, when they found that large-scale emigration won them neither the trade concessions nor the economic credits that they sought? The stick is only valuable when there is also a carrot somewhere in the distance, they point out.

In any event, the Soviets are not some fourth-rate power to be cowed under the pressure of U.S. influence. They will never respond to the either-or threat implicit in linking trade to human rights policy. On the contrary, a hard line freezes both positions and makes it still more difficult to negotiate in favor of emigration. Actually, it might be well to remove Soviet Jewry from the confrontational agenda. Instead, the issue should be entered as a means for relaxing rather than exacerbating tensions.

These two distinct orientations toward the fate of Soviet Jewry are reinforced by a social and organizational logic of their own. By no accident, militant tendencies are associated with grass-roots activists, always clamoring for a more vigorous stance. By contrast, cautions are generally issued by those whose status and perspective place them nearer the top of Jewish organizational life, positions that demand genteel sophistication and diplomacy more than firebrand rhetoric and militant strategies.

Add to this the stake of the U.S. industrial and agricultural communities. From producers of high-tech equipment to farmers interested in exporting grain, there are many who feel that human rights is irrelevant, at best, to good business sense. For them, that means leaving Soviet internal affairs to the Soviets. Less committed to human rights than to their own fiscal well-being, they see trade with the Soviet Union as an important way to sustain the U.S. economic recovery as well as a means of reducing international tensions. To be sure, the same argument was there at the birth of Jackson-Vanik, but several factors have emerged over the past fifteen years that make it particularly potent today.

No longer must we postulate what might result from restrictions on trade with the Soviet Union or how linking trade and human rights might affect Soviet-U.S. relations. There is now substantial data based on practical experience. Within the business community, the experience has all been bad. For example, they argue, the Jackson-Vanik amendment has actually been counterproductive for both U.S. foreign and trade policies. Rather than paralyze Soviet development, it has simply pushed it to new markets where comparable supplies are available without the encumbrances of human rights linkage. The Soviet Union might like U.S. products, but it has learned over the past decade and a half that much of the technology it seeks is readily available elsewhere.

In particular, it is a good bit of diplomatic irony that U.S. allies in Western Europe or the Orient, notably Japan and West Germany, have been far less purist about dealing with Moscow. In addition, there are Soviet goods, for example, liquor, farm equipment, and trucks, that might be popular in the United States except for prohibitive tariffs on exporters not granted most favored nation status, so the U.S. consumer loses as well. All that Jackson-Vanik has done is to remove the Untied States from competition.

Aside from MFN, representatives of commercial interests argue that restricting economic credits hurts the United States as much as it hurts the Soviets. Much of the world's trade is carried out on a credit basis, allowing consumer nations to utilize their currency reserves to remove previous debt and/or to invest in further development. This in turn encourages greater demand and more trade.

It has long been recognized that extending credit to consumers who prove themselves to be good risks serves the purposes of both domestic and international commercial institutions. Unfortunately, some less developed countries that have received substantial credit from Western nations returned the favor by walking the brink of default. The Soviets, however, are an especially good risk. Yet here again, Jackson-Vanik has removed the United States from the market.

Finally, there is the matter of unsettled debts remaining between the United States and the Soviet Union since World War II under the lend-lease program. Washington understood that it would be a hardship to demand repayment immediately after the war from nations that served as its battleground. Indeed, it might undermine the stability of those nations that had been victors. Consequently, the terms of the lease were extended.

These outstanding credits have now been an issue in U.S.-Soviet trade relations for almost four decades. As of the moment, settlement of the debt depends upon normalization of trade relations. This has been interpreted by the Soviet Union to mean the granting of most favored nation status and economic credits. Consequently, aside from the stakes of one or another private sector, the U.S. government has a direct economic interest in facilitating trade.

V

There are two other sets of actors in this international drama, and the script would not be complete without accounting for their positions as well. One is the government of Israel, which was among the initiators of the Soviet Jewry movement in the late 1960s. It is under its auspices that visas are issued for emigrants who leave the Soviet Union. It is Israel, at least initially, that stands as the intended destination for those who emigrate.

The other is a complex of interests posited by Soviet Jews themselves. These include leaders among the immigrant communities in Israel and the United States. Some have been recruited as official or quasi-official spokespeople or lobbyists within the Soviet Jewry movement. Others are operating in a similar capacity inside the Israeli government. Then there are the dissidents and their followers behind the Iron Curtain.

Until recently, there might not have been much to say about the position of the government of Israel regarding Soviet Jewry, apart from what has already been discussed generally. It had an obvious stake in the question of where immigrants would finally reside, and there have been internal differences of administrative concern. But over all, Israeli authorities participated as full, even senior partners in the grand coalition that is the Soviet Jewry movement.

During the latter half of the Peres administration in Jerusalem, however, diplomatic stirrings were felt that might have profound consequences for the movement's future. For the first time in almost twenty years, the Soviet Union indicated quiet but unmistakable interest in renewing diplomatic ties with Israel, broken after the 1967 War. Although not yet consummated, these stirrings have yielded several high-level meetings, and much speculation has followed in their wake.

The Soviets have good reason to want a renewal of diplomatic ties with Israel. As a result of their break, Israel moved still closer toward the United States than it had been before, becoming a virtual U.S. client. It was followed in short order by Egypt, Jordan, and many of the Gulf sheikhdoms, oil embargos of the mid-1970s notwithstanding. The Soviets inherited Syria, Libya, and the PLO—a most unmanageable trio if ever there was one.

The Soviet Union suffered for its identification not only with one side in the Arab-Israel dispute but with its most militant and radical wing. Even within that corner, Moscow was discredited by its actions, or rather inactions, during the Lebanon war of 1982.

In the first case, the easy Israeli victories over the PLO in southern Lebanon and the Syrian forces further inward suggested that their U.S.-made matériel was superior to that supplied by the Soviet Union. The absence of active military support from Moscow at the height of the pounding suggested it was unreliable as a patron and ally.

In fact, the Soviet Union has wanted to regain its credibility as a force in the Middle East for at least a decade. The United States, in a fit of ecumenical spirit, coauthored a communiqué with the Soviet Union on the Middle East in 1977. It may have been the straw that broke the back of Anwar Sadat's camel, for in direct reaction, the late Egyptian president made his historic journey to Jerusalem. He felt that he had been betrayed by the United States and had to seize the initiative himself.

The reaction to such a possibility, in Jerusalem anyway, was much warmer in 1985–86. There is the sense that the peace process has run its course, and the infusion of new blood, even if it is Soviet and Syrian, might allow for new alternatives and options that could not be discussed without these participants. The possibility may also raise new hopes for Jews who reside in the Soviet Union.

As with most such initiatives, its point cuts in two directions. Those within the Israeli government see a renewal of discussions with the Soviet Union as a powerful tool in favor of Jewish emigration. Israel has something the Soviets want and can use it as an incentive to pry loose thousands of Jews. If the Soviets seek a credible role in the Middle East, if they care about normalizing relations with Israel, then they will have to be forthcoming.

The position also affects the self-image of the State of Israel and its relationship with the United States. At bottom, Soviet Jewry is a Jewish issue. It is altogether appropriate that Israel serve as its vanguard. In this way, there may be greater control over the direction of emigration, thus insuring a larger proportion of émigrés who will at least make Israel their first stop.

Further, why should the fate of these dissidents depend upon the good graces of U.S. farmers or business people in linking trade to human rights? On the contrary, neither Israeli foreign policy nor Jewish needs should be captive to even the most munificent outsiders. Israel is not, and world Jewry ought not to be, inherently anti-Soviet. There may be more to gain by negotiation than through the virtual isolation from the Soviet Union characterized by the past two decades.

One further point bears note. If the position was initiated under the administration of Shimon Peres, its chief architect was then-Foreign Minister Yitzhak Shamir. Shamir has now risen to the Premiership according to the rotation agreement struck between the two leaders following Israeli elections of 1984. Both by temperament and by background, Shamir has a greater affinity for the Eastern Bloc than most of his predecessors. He is likely to follow these early encounters during his tenure in office, making rapprochement with the USSR a keystone of foreign policy.

But there are many, both inside the Israeli government and among

leaders of Soviet emigrants, who are less sanguine about the motivations of Moscow and even Jerusalem. Bitterly anti-Soviet, they are not
given to trusting the Soviet Union on any count. Applying rational
models of reasoning to any of their policy needs is a blind pursuit,
they argue. Commitments mean nothing to them, and a negotiating
posture will simply be taken for weakness. The Soviets will have their
way and not release Jews anyway.

Moreover, they wonder aloud, what is the real objective here? Is
the government of Israel entering into discussions with the Soviet Union
in order to gain freedom for Soviet Jews? Or are Soviet Jews once
more to become bait in a diplomatic game that prizes renewed relations more than emigration? If push came to shove, they seem to be
saying, would Israel abandon all or part of its commitment to human
rights behind the Iron Curtain over the fragility of Middle East peace
negotiations? In its most graphic terms, would Israel be willing to
negotiate territory borders on the Golan or the West Bank, for example, in return for large increases in emigration?

Further, it stands to reason that if diplomatic relations were to be
renewed at whatever level, Israelis would have a stake in maintaining
and extending them. They might well ask Jewish dissidents to decrease their activities if it threatened their diplomatic position. In addition, Israel fears a mass emigration that would once more choose the
United States over Israel as its destination. Might it decide that those
who don't come to Israel aren't worth fighting for anyway?

All this is a cruel formulation to be sure, but one that emigrant
leaders worry about. Better, they suggest, that the issue never be raised.
Better that such dark fears languish beneath the surface. Yet the implicit presumption of mistrust seems to extend beyond its obvious targets in Moscow. It redounds, if only in part, toward Jerusalem as
well.

VI

Emigrant leaders have stepped forward on their own. In many ways,
their words and actions bear the stamp of those liberated from a painful and frustrating experience. It also reflects their collective encounter
with Jewish leaders and organizational life since arriving in Israel or
the West.

In the first case, there is a sense that good intentions and staunch commitments aside, it is time for the immigrants to step to the fore. No one understands the needs of the Soviet dissident better than they do, nor can a Westerner comprehend the workings of the Soviet bureaucracy and government. Moralizing and machinations that characterized the past all served their purpose, but activists must now stand aside and allow them to take responsibility for their own.

In addition, many have fresh memories of their first encounters in Israel. They recall the confusion and the bureaucratic difficulties in getting them settled and helping them assimilate. Though their standards of living soon rose, it was a difficult period of adjustment at best.

More troubling, they also recall the many Israelis of North African descent who believed that they had been passed over for benefits and jobs once more. Though they and their parents arrived twenty years earlier, these East European newcomers were getting first choice.

What can you expect, they said resentfully. The Israeli government is populated by children of the same ghettos and shtetlach. They're just taking care of their own. It was an angry and bitter stance that led protestors to carry placards reading: "Let My People Go—Back!"

Finally, emigrants claim that activists tend to satisfy themselves with the spectacular, caring little for the fate of those left behind. It is possible for the Soviet regime to release a few thousand refuseniks, among them some well-known figures, and then crack down on others who have filed to leave. Jobs are lost, benefits rescinded, families divided, as Western protestors pride themselves on those released.

Most important, there has been a significant change in the nature of Jewish life in the Soviet Union. Surely, there are still many who seek to leave for economic and social reasons. But alongside them there has been a genuine renewal of interest in Jewish culture that informs many dissidents. Study groups have emerged around rare teachers of Hebrew, prayers, or classical texts. Ritual objects are hidden and passed along in secret meetings. Writings are circulated that mix political dissent with religious and philosophic thought.

The Soviets have been most strenuous in their attempts to restrict such activities and punish those who participate in them. Teachers have been imprisoned or exiled while their followers fear for their livelihood and their own freedom. Security agents infiltrate study and prayer groups as if they were revolutionary cells. As always, Soviet paranoia is the order of the day.

The sum of it is that emigration isn't the whole story, if indeed it ever was. The quality of life in the Soviet Union for Jews trying to rekindle the spark of their religious and cultural heritage, for Jews who wait to emigrate, is repressive and physically threatening. To pin Soviet diplomatic or trade concessions on the numbers of those allowed to leave is to see only half the story.

To remedy these and other shortcomings, a comprehensive plan has been posited from among the leaders of emigrants here and in Israel. It calls for the prompt release of all Jewish prisoners of conscience, that is, those who have been imprisoned primarily for their dissident activities or their desire to leave the Soviet Union, no matter what the official Soviet charges. These, as well a refuseniks who have been awaiting visas for more than ten years, should be permitted to leave the Soviet Union forthwith.

A second stage of emigration would include all those who have been waiting for permission to leave for more than five years. This would be followed by those refused visas since 1982. The final stage would allow emigration for those applying presently. In all, it is estimated that there are as many as four hundred thousand Soviet Jews who would leave under such a plan.

Interestingly, the plan says nothing about the destination of these new émigrés, something that irks Israeli officials. The key is to get them out, dissidents explain, not to make a Zionist statement. It also ignores the simple fact that were it to be implemented in even its early stages, the numbers of those seeking to leave would immediately inflate. New refuseniks will emerge as they watch their friends and relatives making travel arrangements. Nothing succeeds like success.

Finally, it leaves little for the fine art of diplomacy and discretion that has always marked international relations, especially between and among big powers. There is a genuine and well-founded fear that such diplomacy will leave Soviet Jews behind. The issue is apparently not near the top of the U.S. and Soviet agendas. It seems to lag on the Israeli agenda as well.

All this has the mark of the movement and the problems it faces. In many regards, it has come of age. The excitement of its youth, the rallies, the headline seeking, the pranks, and the impassioned pleas have given way to realpolitik and difficult choices. As is often the case in the process of maturation, there is confusion and disorientation.

There are many things that reside under its control. The direction of protest, access to, and influence in certain aspects of U.S. and Israeli policy are examples. There are many things—trade, diplomacy, or the destinations of new emigrants among them—over which there is little control. Learning to live with such realities is part of growing up.

The questions are tough and numerous. Need there be a conflict between Israeli interests and those of Soviet Jews? Will U.S. Jews have to make a choice between them? Is the purpose of the movement aliyah or simply immigration? Need there be a choice between emigration and amelioration for those who remain behind? Should the new directions for the movement be set by former refuseniks or seasoned leaders from within Jewish organizational and political ranks?

The answers will require lengthy discussion and debate, even as developments in the international arena go on unabated. New directions forged will likely set the tone for the Soviet Jewry movement in the years to come. They can insulate believers and refuseniks as their fates are thrashed about in the stormy seas of global politics, or they can place them right in the thick of things as the human rights issue is debated along with trade and diplomacy at the highest international levels.

Most important, they can stem the sense that there is little clear strategy emerging from either Washington or Jerusalem. Increasingly, the movement is realizing that its own initiative is its best friend, no matter who sits at the helm. The demand is a heady but necessary task. For of all frustrations, there is none worse than being caught short.

Bibliography

BOOKS, MONOGRAPHS, AND SPECIAL PUBLICATIONS

Abramov, S. Zalman, ed. Understanding One Another: An Israeli Perspective. New York: American Jewish Committee, 1984.

Aviner, S. H. Clarifications on the Matter of "And They Shall Not Rise as a Wall" (in Hebrew). Jerusalem: Noam, 1980.

Avineri, Shlomo. The Making of Modern Zionism. New York: Schocken Books, 1984.

Avruch, Kevin. American Immigrants in Israel. Chicago: University of Chicago Press, 1981.

Barakat, Halim. Lebanon in Strife. Austin: University of Texas, 1977.

Baron, Salo. The Russian Jew Under Tsars and Soviets. New York: Macmillan, 1976.

Baum, Phil. Noshrim: The Current Dilemma. New York: American Jewish Congress, 1980.

Benvenisti, Meron. The West Bank Data Project. Washington, D.C.: American Enterprise, 1984.

Bowker, G., ed. Race and Ethnic Relations. New York: Holmes and Meier, 1976.

Brown, Charles, and Paula Hyman. Jewish Women in America. New York: New American Library, 1977.

Bulka, Reuven. Dimensions of Orthodox Judaism. New York: Ktav, 1983.

Cohen, Amnon. Political Parties on the West Bank Under the Jordanian Regime, 1949–1967. Ithaca: Cornell University Press, 1982.

Cohen, Naomi. American Jews and the Zionist Idea. New York: Ktav, 1975.

Cohen, Steven. Attitudes of American Jews Toward Israel and Israelis. New York: American Jewish Committee, 1983.

———. The 1984 National Survey of American Jews. New York: American Jewish Committee, 1985.

Cohen, Steven, and Paula Hyman, eds. Perspectives on the Jewish Family. New York: Holmes and Meier, 1984.

Cohen, Steven, and Paul Ritterband. Greater New York Jewish Population Study. New York: Federation of Jewish Philanthropies, 1983.

Curtis, Michael, and Mordecai Chertoff. Israel: Social Structure and Change. New Brunswick, N.J.: Transaction, 1973.

Davis, Moshe. Zionism in Transition. New York: Herzl, 1980.

Elazar, Daniel, ed. Community and Polity. Philadelphia: Jewish Publication Society, 1976.

———. Governing People and Territories. Philadelphia: Institute for the Study of Human Issues, 1982.

Feingold, Henry. Zion in America. New York: Twayne, 1975.

Flappen, Simha. Zionism and the Palestinians. New York: Barnes and Noble, 1979.

Gilbert, Martin. Jews of Hope. New York: Viking, 1985.

Gitelman, Zvi. Becoming Israelis: Political Resocialization of Soviet and American Immigrants. New York: Praeger, 1982.

Gittler, Joseph. Jewish Life in the United States. New York: New York University Press, 1981.

Glazer, Nathan. American Judaism. 2nd ed. Chicago: University of Chicago Press, 1972.

Glazer, Nathan, and Daniel Moynihan. Beyond the Melting Pot. Cambridge: MIT Press, 1970.

———. Ethnicity: Theory and Experience. Cambridge: Harvard University Press, 1975.

Gold, Bertram, ed. Understanding One Another: Excerpts of a Discussion on American Jewish Israel Relations. New York: American Jewish Committee, 1983.

Goldscheider, Calvin. Jewish Continuity and Change. Bloomington: Indiana University Press, 1985.

Greely, Andrew. Ethnicity in the United States. New York: Wiley, 1974.

Greenberg, Blu. On Women and Judaism. Philadelphia: Jewish Publication Society, 1981.

Harris, Louis, and Bert Swanson. Black-Jewish Relations in New York City. New York: Praeger, 1970.

Heilman, Samuel. People of the Book. Chicago: University of Chicago Press, 1983.

Helmreich, William. The World of the Yeshiva. New York: Free Press, 1982.

Hertzberg, Arthur. The Zionist Idea. New York: Atheneum, 1975.

———. Being Jewish in America. New York: Schocken Books, 1978.

Howe, Irving. World of Our Fathers. New York: Harcourt Brace Jovanovich, 1976.

Isaac, Rael. Israel Divided. Baltimore: Johns Hopkins University Press, 1976.

Issacs, Stephen. Jews and American Politics. Garden City, N.Y.: Doubleday, 1974.

Kedourie, Elie, and Sylvia Hyam. Zionism and Arabism in Palestine and Israel. London: Cass, 1982.

Kochan, L. Jews in Soviet Russia Since 1917. New York: Oxford University Press, 1978.

Koltun, E., ed. Jewish Women: A New Perspective. New York: Schocken Books, 1976.

Korey, William. The Soviet Case: Anti-Semitism in Russia. New York: Viking Press, 1973.

Laquer, Walter. A History of Zionism. New York: Holt, Rinehart and Winston, 1972.

Lendvai, Paul. Anti-Semitism Without Jews. New York: Doubleday, 1971.

Levin, Nora. While Messiah Tarried: Jewish Socialist Movements, 1871–1917. New York: Schocken Books, 1977.

Levine, Naomi, and Martin Hochbaum. Poor Jews: An American Awakening. New Brunswick, N.J.: Transaction, 1974.

Liebman, Charles. The Ambivalent American Jew. Philadelphia: Jewish Publication Society, 1973.

———. Aspects of the Religious Behavior of American Jews. New York: Ktav, 1975.

———. Pressure Without Sanctions: The Influence of World Jewry on Israeli Policy. Rutherford, N.J.: Fairleigh Dickenson, 1977.

Liebman, Charles, and Eliezer Don-Yehiya. Religion and Politics in Israel. Bloomington: Indiana University Press, 1984.

Linzer, Norman. The Jewish Family: Authority and Tradition in Modern Times. New York: Human Sciences, 1984.

Mahler, Gregory. Readings on the Israeli Political System. Washington, D.C.: University Press, 1982.

Malachy, Yona. American Fundamentalism and Israel. Atlantic Highlands, N.J.: Humanities Press, 1978.

Mayer, Egon. Love and Tradition: Marriage Between Jews and Christians. New York: Plenum, 1985.

Mayer, Egon, and Carl Shengold. Intermarriage and the Jewish Future. New York: American Jewish Committee, 1979.

Miller, Jack. Jews in Soviet Culture. New Brunswick, N.J.: Transaction, 1983.

Monson, Rela. Jewish Campus Life: A Survey of Student Attitudes Toward Marriage and Family. New York: American Jewish Committee, 1984.

Nadel, Max, ed. Portrait of the American Jew. New York: Barron's, 1978.

Newman, David, ed. The Impact of Gush Emunim. London: Croom Helm, 1985.

Orbach, William. The American Movement to Aid Soviet Jewry. Amherst: University of Massachusetts Press, 1979.

Peretz, Don. The Middle East Today. New York: Holt, Rinehart and Winston, 1977.

Peters, Joan. From Time Immemorial. New York: Harper and Row, 1984.

Pipes, Daniel. In the Path of God: Islam and Political Power. New York: Basic Books, 1983.

Reichman, Shalom, Non-Agricultural Jewish Settlement in Judea and Samaria (in Hebrew). Jerusalem: Hebrew University Press, 1981.

Rubinstein, Amnon. The Zionist Dream Revisited. New York: Schocken Books, 1984.

Sachar, Howard M. A History of Israel. New York: Knopf, 1976.

Schnall, David. Radical Dissent in Contemporary Israeli Politics: Cracks in the Wall. New York: Praeger, 1979.

———. Beyond the Green Line: Israeli Settlements West of the Jordan. New York: Praeger, 1984.

Scholem, Gershon. On Jews and Judaism. New York: Schocken Books, 1977.

Silberman, Charles. A Certain People. New York: Simon and Schuster, 1985.

Sklare, Marshall. The Jew in American Society. New York: Behrman House, 1974.

———. The Jews: Social Patterns of an American Group. Westport, Conn.: Greenwood Press, 1977.

———. Understanding American Jewry. New Brunswick, N.J.: Transaction, 1982.

Smith, Hanoch. Attitude of Israelis Toward America and American Jews. New York: American Jewish Committee, 1983.

Sowell, Thomas. Markets and Minorities. New York: Basic Books, 1981.

———. Ethnic America. New York: Basic Books, 1983.

Vargo, Bela. Jewish Assimilation in Modern Times. Boulder, Colo.: Westview, 1981.

Yankelovich, Daniel. Anti-Semitism in the United States. New York: American Jewish Committee, 1981.

JOURNALS, MAGAZINES, AND PERIODICALS

Amrani, Israel. "David's Dream." Jerusalem Post, August 4, 1982.

Brinker, M. "The End of Zionism?" Dissent 32 (Winter 1985):77–82.

Chenkin, Alvin, and Fred Massarik. "The United States National Jewish Population Survey." American Jewish Yearbook 73 (1972): 264–306.

Chenkin, Alvin, and Gary Tobin. "Recent Jewish Community Population Studies." American Jewish Yearbook 85 (1985):154–78.

Cohen, Steven. "American Jewish Feminism: A Story in Conflicts and Compromises." American Behavioral Scientist 23 (March 1980):519–58.

———. "The 1981–82 National Survey of American Jews." American Jewish Yearbook 83 (1983):89–110.

Cohen, Steven, and Leonard Fein. "From Integration to Survival: American Jewish Anxieties in Transition." The Annals 480 (July 1985):75–88.

Davis, Moshe, and Ernest Stock, eds. "Israel's Place in World Jewry: Changing Perspectives." Forum (Special Section) 54/55 (Spring/Summer 1985), 57/58 (Winter/Spring 1985–86) and 59 (Summer, 1986).

Dror, Yeheskel. "A Guide Through the Perplexities of Israeli Politics After Begin." Political Quarterly 55 (March 1984):38–47.

Della Pergola, S. "Patterns of American Jewish Fertility." Demography 17 (August 1980):261–73.

Dulzin, Aryeh. "Zionism vs. Pro-Israelism?" Forum 38 (Summer 1980):65–78.

Elazar, Daniel. "Transforming the Thrust of the Zionist Movement to Preserve its Spirit." Forum 51/52 (Spring/Summer 1984):1–11.

Elizur, Dov. "Israelis in the United States: Motives, Attitudes, and Intentions." American Jewish Yearbook 80 (1980):53–67.

Fein, Aharon. "The Rate of Emigration from Israel." Forum 53 (Fall 1984):53–60.

Fein, Leonard. "Liberalism and the American Jews." Midstream 19 (October 1973): 3-18.

Gilboa, Eytan. "Attitudes of American Jewry Toward the Arab-Israel Conflict." Forum 57/58 (Winter/Spring 1985):57–72.

Goldschieder, Calvin, and Dov Friedlander. "Religiosity Patterns in Israel." American Jewish Yearbook 83 (1983):3–39.

Goldstein, Sidney. "Jews in the United States: Perspectives from Demography." American Jewish Yearbook 81 (1981):3–59.

Gruen, George. "United States and Israel: The Impact of the Lebanon War." American Jewish Yearbook 84 (1984):73–103.

Himmelfarb, Harold. "Agents of Religious Socialization among American Jews." Sociological Quarterly 20 (August 1979):477–94.

Hochbaum, Jerry. "Who is a Jew: A Sociological Perspective." Tradition 14 (Spring/Summer 1973):35–41.

———. "American Orthodoxy." Tradition 15 (Spring 1974):5–14.

Horowitz, Irving Louis. "The Politics of Centrism." Forum 38 (Summer 1980):31–42.

Lamm, Norman. "The Ideology of Neturei Karta: According to the Satmerer Version." Tradition 12 (Fall 1971):43–50.

Lazerwitz, Bernard. "American Jewish Denominations: A Social and Religious Profile." American Sociological Review 44 (August 1979):656–66.

———. "Past and Future Trends in the Size of American Jewish Denominations." Journal of Reform Judaism 26 (Summer 1979):77–82.

Levine, Etan. "A Critique of Criticism." Forum 46/47 (Fall/Winter 1982):47–60.

Lustick, Ian. "Zionism and the State of Israel." Middle East Studies 16 (January 1980):127–46.

Mandel, Ralph. "Israel in 1982: The War in Lebanon." American Jewish Yearbook 84 (1984):3–72.

Maller, Allen. "Mixed Marriage and Reform Rabbis." Judaism 24 (Winter 1975):48–49.

Mayer, Egon. "Jewish Orthodoxy in America." Journal of Jewish Sociology 15 (December 1973):151–65.

———. "Processes and Outcomes in Marriages Between Jews and Non-Jews." American Behavioral Scientist, 23 (March 1980):487–518.

Mouly, R. W. "Israel: Darling of the Religious Right." Humanist 42 (May 1982):5–11.

Reisman, Bernard. "Americans in Israeli: Conflict on a Moshav." Forum 46/47 (Fall/Winter 1982):201–12.

Rosenfield, Gary. "Attitudes Toward American Jews." Public Opinion Quarterly 46 (Fall 1982):431–43.

Schenker, Avraham. "Zionism in Distress." Forum 46/47 (Fall/Winter 1982):7–24.

Schmelz, U. O. "Jewish Survival: The Demographic Factors." American Jewish Yearbook 81 (1981):61–117.

Schnall, David. "Yored is also a Noun." Midstream 24 (February 1978):73–78.

———. "Religion, Ideology, and Dissent in Contemporary Israeli Politics." Tradition 15 (Summer 1979):13–34.

———. "Soviet Jewry: Malaise in the Movement." Midstream 26 (March 1980):8–13.

———. "Orthodoxy Resurgent." Judaism 30 (Fall 1981):460–6.

————. "American Zionism: Continuity and Change." Tradition 18 (Summer 1982):119–27.

Schwartz, Arnold. "Intermarriage in the United States." American Jewish Yearbook 71 (1972):101–21.

Shamir, M., and John Sullivan. "Jews and Arabs in Israel." Journal of Conflict Resolution 29 (June 1985):283–305.

Shapiro, Leon. "Soviet Jewry Since the Death of Stalin." American Jewish Yearbook 79 (1979):77–103.

Shmueli, Ephraim. "Israel, Galut, and Zionism." Judaism 23 (Summer 1974):264–75.

Sklare, Marshall. "Intermarriage and Jewish Survival." Commentary 49 (March 1970):51–60.

Tabory, Ephraim. "Reform and Conservative Judaism in Israel: A Social and Religious Profile." American Jewish Yearbook 83 (1983):41–61.

Tempkin, Sefton. "A Century of Reform Judaism in America." American Jewish Yearbook 74 (1975):3–75.

Verbit, Mervin. "Jewish Identity and the Israel-Diaspora Dialogue." Forum 48 (Spring 1983):63–74.

Waxman, Chaim. "The Centrality of Israel in American Jewish Life." Judaism 25 (Spring 1976):175–87.

————. "The Threadbare Canopy: Vicissitudes of the Jewish Family in Modern American Society." American Behavioral Scientist 23 (March 1980):467–86.

Woocher, Jonathan. "The American Jewish Polity in Transition." Forum 47 (Fall/Winter 1982):1–70.

Index

Abortion, 61
Affirmative action, 55
Afghanistan, 157
Age, median, 10-11; *see also* Elderly
Agudath Yisrael, 34
Aliyah, 88-89; Americans and, 85-99, 129-130; Soviet Jews and, 159-161, 165-166, 166-168, 168-169, 170-171
American Council for Judaism, 122
American Jewish Committee, surveys by, 6n, 20n; anti-Semitism, 123-124; support for Israel, 122-123
American Jewish Yearbook, 6n
American Jews and Israel: Aliyah and, 85-99; commitment to, 126-131, 134-135; fund raising, 127-128; Israel as source of identity, 122-127
Amrani, Israel, 99n
Anti-Semitism in the United States (Yankelovitch), 123n
Anti-Semitism, survey on, 123–124

Arabs, 77, 81, 84, 101-117; Israeli dilemma and, 111-115, 116-117; moderate, 103-104, 105-106, 107-111; PLO and, 104-107, 110-111; refugees, 115-116; West Bank and, 101-105, 107-111
Arafat, Yassir, 73, 104-105, 107
Armaments: in Middle East, 58-60, 166; reduction talks, 156, 158
Attitudes of American Jews Toward Israel and Israelis (Cohen), 122n
Aviner, S. H., 72n
Avineri, Shlomo, 112

Ba'alei Teshuva, 37-39, 46
Bayh, Birch, 63
Bethlehem, 80, 97, 101
Birth control, 10
Birthrate, Jewish, 6-7, 9, 11, 14-15, 132
Black-Jewish relations, 55-57
Black September, 115
Bonner, Yelena, 158
Breira, 19
Brezhnev, Leonid, 154

Carlebach, Rabbi Shlomo, 37
Carlin, George, 47
Carter, Jimmy, 60
Castle Garden, 4
Chabad, 37
Charry, Rabbi Marim, 148
Child rearing, 9-10, 15-16; *see also*
Israelis in the U.S.
Christian fundamentalism, 40; attitudes toward Israel and, 61-62, 134; missionary activities of, 61-63; politics and, 61-62, 63; theology and, 61-62
Church, Frank, 63
Civil rights movement, 55
Clarification on the Matter of "And They Shall Not Rise as a Wall," (Aviner), 72n
Cohen, Steven, 6n, 122n
Congress, U.S., 63, 155-156
Conservative Judaism, 33-34, 45, 48-49
Conservative politics in U.S., 57-58, 134; Christian fundamentalism and, 61-62, 63
Conversion to Judaism: intermarriage and, 21-23, 28-29; Israeli law and, 75-76; Reform Judaism and, 23, 75-76
Conversion to Orthodox Judaism, *see* Ba'alei Teshuva
Cults, 40

Debs, Eugene V., 53
Democratic party: Blacks and, 55-57; Jews and, 51, 53-54, 57, 63-64
Demography, Jewish, in U.S., 6-7, 132-133; *see also* Birthrate
Détente, 153-154, 155
Diaspora, 35, 129-130

Eastern European Jews, 4-5, 33, 35-36, 45, 88
Education: higher, 5, 25-26; religious, 37, 38, 41-43, 45-6; *see also Kolel*
Egypt, 102-103, 106, 166
El-David, 98-99
Elderly, 10-15, 62, 132
Elections, Jewish voting in, 133-134; *see also* Presidential elections
Electoral college, 133-134
Ellis Island, 4
Esses, Elia, 158
Evangelism, *see* Christian fundamentalism

Family: size, 9-10; values, 8, 12, 15-16
Farrakhan, Louis, 56-57, 64
Foreign policy, U.S., *see* U.S. foreign policy
Forward, 52-53
Fundamental Christianity, *see* Christian fundamentalism
Fund raising, 127-128

Gahelet, 147-149
Gaza Strip, 106, 109, 113
Geneva summit, 158
German Jews, 32, 45
Gorbachev, Mikhail, 158
Great Britain, 107, 112
Greater New York Conference on Soviet Jewry, 153n
Greater New York Jewish Population Study (Ritterband and Cohen), 6n
Gush Emunim, 77-82, 83-84

Haifa, 91
Halakah, see Jewish law
Haredim, 71-73, 75, 82-84; *see also* Neturei Karta

Hasidic Jews, 34, 35, 38, 45; in Israel, 67-73; *see also* Haredim
Hebrew Union College, 33
Hebron, 79, 80, 81, 96, 101
Herod, King, 97
Herodian, 97-98
Holocaust, 35, 127; survivors in U.S., 35-36
Human rights linked to trade, 156, 158, 164, 167
Hungary, 157
Hussein, King, 109, 115
Huzander, Sheikh, 106

Immigrants in U.S., 3-5, 31-34, 52-54; Israeli, 137-152; Soviet Jews, 159-162
Immigration to Israel, *see* Aliyah
Income, 5, 9-10, 15
Intermarriage, 18-29, 39-40, 133; children of, 23-24; conversion and, 21, 23, 28-29; rates of, 20-21; religious affiliation and, 21-22, 40
Intermarriage and the Jewish Future (Mayer and Shengold), 20n
Iran, 60, 84, 106-107, 115, 157
Israel, State of, 35, 42, 83; American Jewish commitment to, 121-123, 126--131, 134-135; Arabs in West Bank, 101-104, 107-111, 113-115; Black attitudes toward, 55-56; Christian fundamentalist attitudes toward, 61-62, 134; emigration from, 131-132, 137-152; invasion of Lebanon by, 58-59, 105; Jewish settlements in West Bank and, 77-82, 109-110; Palestinian Arabs and, 111-115, 116-117; religious opposition to, 68-74, 82-84; Six Day War (1967) and, 80, 102, 103, 104, 154, 166;

source of ethnic identity, 122-127; Soviet Jews and, 154-155, 159-161, 165-171; Soviet Union and, 159, 166-169; status of non-Orthodox practices in, 75-6; U.S. Jewish settlements and, 86, 87-88, 91-99; U.S. policy toward, 58-60, 128-129; U.S. politics and, 57-58, 63, 121-123, 124-125, 133-135
Israelis in the U.S., 131-132, 137-152; child rearing and, 144-147; culture clubs and, 147-149; disaffection with Israel, 142-144; economic mobility and, 138-142; renewed religious ties, 142-143

Jackson, Henry, 155
Jackson, Jesse, 55-57, 64
Jackson-Vanik, 155-159, 163-165
Jerusalem, 52, 67, 77, 80, 91, 93, 109
Jerusalem Post, 99n
Jewish law, in Israel, 75-76, 83
Jordan, 101-104, 108-109, 115
Judea, 77, 85-86, 88, 90-91, 96, 125

Karnei Shomron, 92-93
Kedumim, 77
Kolel, 43, 93-95
Kook, Rabbi Zvi Yehuda, 78-79
Kosher establishments, 36-37, 41

Labor movement in U.S., 52-53, 54
Lebanon, 102-103, 105, 114-115; Israeli invasion of, 58-60, 116, 166; Palestinians and, 115-16
Levinger, Rabbi Moshe, 78-79
Liberalism, political: Blacks and, 55-57; Jews and, 51-55, 63-64
Libya, 59, 106, 115, 166

Love and Tradition: Marriage Between Jews and Christians (Mayer), 20n

Maaleh Amos, 93-95
Markets and Minorities (Sowell), 5n
Marriage: Orthodox practices and, 43, 46; popular image of Jewish men and women in, 24-25; postponement of, 7-9, 14; *see also* intermarriage
Matchmaker, 9
Mayer, Egon, 20n
Meah Shearim, 68
Medical care, 11-12
Men, Jewish, in U.S.: education, 5; popular image of, 24-25
Mendelevich, Yosef, 158
Messiah and divine redemption of Israel, 71-72, 78, 83
Mondale, Walter, 56, 57
Moshav, 95
Most favored nation (MFN) status, 155-157, 164-165

Nablus (Shechem), 77-78, 101; *see also* West Bank
Nation of Islam, 56
National Conference on Soviet Jewry, 153n
National Survey of American Jews (Cohen), 6n
Neighborhoods, Jewish, 11-12, 13, 36-37, 132-133
Neturei Karta, 68-70, 73; *see also* Haredim
New York City, 4, 11, 38, 53, 138
Nicaragua, 60
Non-Agricultural Jewish Settlement in Judea and Samaria (Reichman), 86n

Organizations, Jewish, 7, 15, 34, 39, 44-45, 48; *see also* Synagogues
Orlov, Yuri, 158
Orthodox Judaism in U.S., 35-49; communities, 36-37, 43-44; relations with non-Orthodox, 44-45; religious right and, 41-44; return to, 37-39; revitalization of 35-37, 39-40; stratification among, 44-47
Orthodox settlements in Israel, 92-96

Palestine Liberation Organization (PLO), 59, 73, 104-107, 109-110, 115-117
Palestinian Arabs, *see* Arabs
Pan-Arabism, 102-103
People's Republic of China, 157
Peres, Shimon, 117, 166, 167
Pittsburgh Platform, 122
Politics in Israel: Gush Emunim and, 81-82, 83-84; Palestinian Arabs and, 113-117; religious opposition to the State, 68-74, 82-84; wars and, 58-59, 80
Politics in U.S., Jews and, 51-58; blacks, 55-57; Christian fundamentalists, 61-63, 134-135; Israel as an issue, 121-123, 125; liberalism, 51-55, 63-64; voting and, 133-134
Popular Front for the Liberation of Palestine, 106
Prayer in school, 61
Prayer services, 37, 41
Presidential elections, 53, 55, 58, 63, 121-122, 158
Prisoners of conscience, 170
Professional occupations, 5-6, 36-37, 43, 54-55
Protestantism, intermarriage and, 18-

19, 21; *see also* Christian fundamentalism

Quotas, 36, 54

Radical Dissent in Contemporary Israeli Politics (Schnall), 73n
Rainbow coalition, 56, 64
Reagan, Ronald, 57-58, 60-61, 63, 128, 157-158
Reform Judaism: intermarriage and, 23, 32-33, 49; patrilineal descent, 75-76
Refugee camps, Arab, 103-104, 105, 115-116
Refuseniks, 155, 169-170
Reichman, Shalom, 86n
Religious practices in U.S.: assimilation and, 31-33, 39-40; conversion and, 21-22; differences among Orthodox Jews, 44-48; intermarriage and, 26-29 Orthodox Jews and, 36-39, 41-42
Religious renewal in U.S., 39-42; *see also* Ba'alei Teshuva
Religious Zionism, *see* Gush Emunim
Republican party, 53, 57-58, 60-61, 63
Retirement, 11-12, 13
Riskin, Rabbi Shlomo, 37
Ritterband, Paul, 6n
Roosevelt, Franklin D., 53
Rosenfeld, David, 97-99

Sabbath, 36, 43, 73, 74-75
Sadat, Anwar, 166-167
Sakharov, Andrei, 158
Samaria, 77, 85-86, 88, 90-91, 92-93, 96, 125
Sandinista government, 60
Sarbanes, Paul, 63

Schnall, David, 73n
Senate, U.S., 63
Senior citizens, *see* Elderly
Settlements, Jews in West Bank, 77-82, 85-86, 88, 90-99
Shadchan, see Matchmaker
Shamir, Yitzhak, 167
Shcharansky, Anatoly, 158
Shechem, *see* Nablus
Shengold, Carl, 6n
Shtetl, 4, 31, 52
Singles, 8-9, 46-47
Six Day War (1967), 80, 102-103, 104, 154, 166
Socialism, 35, 52-53
Soviet Jews: emigration from Soviet Union, 154-159, 162, 166-171; immigration to U.S., 159-162; in Soviet Union, 153-155, 169-170; Israel and, 159-161, 165-171; *see also* Jackson-Vanik
Sowell, Thomas, 5n
Stevenson, Adlai, 156
Strategic Arms Limitation Talks (SALT), 157
Sunbelt, migration to, 11-12, 132-133, 134
Surveys of Jews in U.S.: age, 10-11; anti-Semitism, 123-124; birth control, 10; education, 5; family size, 6-7; professional occupations, 5-6; support for Israel, 122-123; synagogue affiliation, 22, 124
Swaggert, Jimmy, 61
Synagogues, 7, 22, 39, 124, 147-149; Orthodox, 48-49; Reform, 32-34
Syria, 59, 103, 106-107, 115-116

Tekoah, 97
Tel Aviv, 77, 91-92

Temple Israel of Great Neck, 147-149

Terrorism, Arab, 60, 96-99, 106-107, 128-129

Trade Act of 1974, 155-156; *see also* Jackson-Vanik

Trade between U.S. and USSR., 153-159, 163-165, 167

Tripoli, 107

Tunisia, 107

Union of American Hebrew Congregations, 33

Union of Soviet Socialist Republics: change in leadership, 158; Jewish emigration linked to trade with U.S., 155-159, 163-165; Middle East and, 59-60, 106, 117, 128, 159, 166-167; renewal of ties with Israel, 155-159, 163-165, 166-169

United Nations, 101, 105, 107, 115

U.S. foreign policy, 60-61; Israel and, 58-60, 128-129, 166-167; Soviet Union and, 153-159, 163-165, 167; terrorism and, 60, 107

Vanik, Charles, 155

Washington Post, 76

West Bank, 77-82, 125; Americans in, 85-86, 88, 90-99; Arabs in, 101-105, 107-111, 113-114

"Who is a Jew?", 75-76

Women, Jewish: career vs. family, 9-10, 15; childbearing, 9-10; education, 5; Hasidic, 67-68; marriage, 7-9, 43; popular image of, 24-25

Yankelovich, Daniel, 123n

Yeshiva University, 37

Yishuv, 85, 88, 91, 95, 98

Yishuv kehilati, 92-96

Yom Kippur War (1973), 80, 138

Yordim, 131, 137-152

Young Israel, 34

Zamed, 106

Zionism, 33, 35-36, 61; American aliyah and, 85-99; American Jewish support for Israel and, 122-123, 124-127, 129-130, 134-135; conflict with Soviet Jewry, 159-162, 170-171; Gush Emunim and, 77-82, 83-84; Messiah and divine redemption, 71-72, 78, 79, 83; Palestinian Arabs and, 110-112; religious opposition to, 68-74, 82-84

About the Author

DAVID J. SCHNALL is Professor on the Faculty of Business, Public Administration, and Accountancy at Long Island University and Adjunct Professor at the Wurzweiler School of Social Work, Yeshiva University. He holds a Ph.D. in political science from Fordham University and was ordained a rabbi at Yeshiva University. A prolific writer and critic, Dr. Schnall is the author of *Beyond the Green Line: Israeli Settlements West of the Jordan* (New York: Praeger, 1984), *Radical Dissent in Contemporary Israeli Politics: Cracks in the Wall* (New York: Praeger, 1979), and *Ethnicity and Suburban Local Politics* (New York: Praeger, 1975). He is coeditor of *Contemporary Issues in Health Care* (New York: Praeger, 1984) and has written over forty articles, essays, and reviews dealing with U.S. public policy, Jewish affairs, and the Middle East. Dr. Schnall is a well-known lecturer who has addressed audiences at universities and community centers throughout the country. A frequent guest on local television and radio talk programs, he has also contributed features and commentary to several news publications.